# PREACHING
## TO
# HEAD AND HEART

## THOMAS R. SWEARS

Abingdon Press
Nashville

PREACHING TO HEAD AND HEART

*Copyright © 2000 by Abingdon Press*

**Library of Congress Cataloging-in-Publication Data**

Swears, Thomas R., 1946–
    Preaching to head and heart / Thomas R. Swears.
        p.   cm.
    Includes bibliographical references.
    ISBN 0-687-06830-4 (alk. paper)
        1. Preaching.   I. Title.

BV4211.2 .S92    2000
251—dc21                                                        99-049219

Scripture quotations, unless otherwise indicated, are from the New Revised Standard Version Bible, copyright © 1989, by the Division of Christian Education of the National Council of the Churches of Christ in the United States of America.

Scripture quotations noted KJV are from the King James Version of the Bible.

Scripture quotations noted RSV are from the Revised Standard Version of the Bible, copyright 1946, 1952, 1971 by the Division of Christian Education of the National Council of the Churches of Christ in the USA. Used by permission.

00 01 02 03 04 05 06 07 08 09—10 9 8 7 6 5 4 3 2 1

MANUFACTURED IN THE UNITED STATES OF AMERICA

*For Linda, who is my music,*
*my own heart's sweetest song,*
*my loveliest, dearest thought.*

*ઝ৸*

Lord, might I be but as a saw,
A plane, a chisel, in thy hand!—
No, Lord! I take it back in awe,
Such prayer for me is far too grand,
I pray, O Master, let me lie,
As on thy bench the favored wood;
Thy saw, thy plane, thy chisel ply
And work me into something good.

—GEORGE MACDONALD
*Diary of an Old Soul*

# CONTENTS

# Acknowledgments

Once, in a moment of seminary student angst, I fled to the comfort of my dearly loved New Testament professor, Jacob Heikkinen, looking for some way out of my confusion, despair, and self-loathing because I didn't seem to have an original idea in my head. It was somewhat reassuring to me to see his office in considerable disarray, with books, journals, student papers, and an assortment of other personal articles strewn haphazardly about. Dr. Heikkinen soon sensed the reason for my being there and in his Finnish wisdom used the material at hand to teach me a lesson. "Oh, aren't these items strewn about a metaphor for life," he said. "They remind us of the order we seek and the chaos in which finally we live." This was, I suppose now, both a word of counsel to me and an excuse for the condition of his study. But then he went on to say that for most of us creativity consists in seeing the old discovered truths in a new light, of making some personal sense of what we have read, of what others have taught us, in a way that rings true in our own hearts and minds. Creativity, he said, was not always discovering something new or saying something that has never been said before, but rather speaking what is already well known from the unique center of your own life and experience. Or, as I've heard Fred Craddock put it, reflecting over the already known is the highest form of learning.

9

Acknowledgments

Dr. Heikkinen was a saving grace to me and over all the years since has helped me to remember, cherish, and honor the gifts my mentors and teachers have so freely shared with me. Neither this book nor my previous book, *The Approaching Sabbath: Spiritual Disciplines for Pastors*, would have been possible without the unselfish and loving gifts of my teachers. Chief among these is Fred B. Craddock, surely one of America's finest Christian teachers and preachers. I have yet to fully calculate my debt to him. His scholar's insight and pastor's heart suffuse my own thought and writing. In this book, I am particularly in his debt for the sound method of sermon preparation he has taught me and thousands of other preachers. Less well known perhaps is another of my teachers, J. Phillip Swander, who died before his helpful work on the "how" of sermon delivery reached a very broad audience. I am in his debt for his sound and practical counsel on the themes of curiosity, valuing the listener, and partnering developed here. Fred Craddock deepened my passion for preaching, and Phillip Swander tutored me in how it can best be done. Each has demonstrated in his own preaching and teaching a deep commitment to and understanding of the importance of both the head and the heart in Christian proclamation. I owe them both a debt I am not equal to repaying. It is my hope that this book will be, in some small way, an expression of my gratitude and a modest albeit heartfelt down payment.

I am further grateful for the generous support and encouragement of the people of the Lutheran Church of the Good Shepherd and particularly for the work of my typist, Nancy Koch.

Finally, I am grateful for the love of my wife, Linda, and the joy of our daughter, Mollie. Without them, the journey between my own head and heart would be a much, much longer one indeed.

# FOREWORD

ॐ

All of us who regularly preach will agree that each week we undertake a journey that involves our heads and our hearts. We may identify the longest part of that journey differently. For some of us the longest journey is from the head to the heart, for others it is from the heart to the head, for still others it is from the head and heart to the mouth. However it is that we identify the longest part of the journey, we know that the journey itself is arduous and requires both discipline and courage. Often the journey is so arduous that we fail to complete it. We journey only from study to pulpit, leaving our minds and hearts separate and disengaged. When such disengagement occurs, the loss to preacher and congregation is severe.

Tom Swears understands a great deal about the preacher's journey, its barriers, demands, and variations. In this volume he offers encouragement so that the journey between head and heart can be made and so that it can be made intentionally, faithfully, compassionately, and well. His purpose is to help preachers connect their own heads and hearts and to better equip them to connect the hearts and heads of their listeners. The goal is preaching that nurtures both preacher and listener in the capacity "to see the extraordinary presence of God in the ordinary events of their lives," to

11

acknowledge both the presence of Christ beyond their knowing and the presence of Christ among them.

The encouragement offered here is a stimulating mix of substance and passion, of cognitive learnings and reflection on pastoral experience. The author is an enthusiastic, dependable fellow-traveler and guide. Along the way, he points out the connection between the head, heart, and ministerial authority. He recognizes sermon listeners as valued participants in the preaching act and creates space for their hearts and minds to respond. He urges a healthy and harmonious balance between speech and silence, both in the pulpit and out of it. He leaves ample room for untidiness, mystery, and humility, allowing preachers to dare to speak the truth as they have come to know it.

Readers of this volume will meet many who have been part of Tom Swears' own journey from head to heart related to preaching. There are theologians, biblical scholars, teachers, homileticians, preachers, divines, writers of fiction, students of narrative, poets, and chroniclers of the spirit. It makes for a rich camaraderie. Yet one of the chief benefits for readers is meeting Tom Swears himself. He is a disciplined, compassionate, and honest preacher who represents well D. H. Lawrence's definition of thought: "A man in his wholeness wholly attending."

**Richard L. Thulin**
Lutheran Theological Seminary
Gettysburg, Pennsylvania

# PREFACE

જીરુ

O world, Thou choosest not the better part!
It is not wisdom to be only wise,
And on the inward vision close the eyes;
But it is wisdom to believe the heart.

GEORGE SANTAYANA
"O World, Thou Choosest Not the Better Part"

Even the pastor who lives in the parsonage right next door to the church needs to prepare for a long journey every week. And so do all the rest of us who preach. It is the journey connecting the head to the heart. The purpose of this book is to encourage the men and women who make that journey every Sunday and to help them do so intentionally, faithfully, and well, both for their own spiritual well-being and for that of the people who listen to the sermons they preach.

Frederick Buechner has wisely counseled preachers that "not to speak from the heart of where their faith comes from is to risk never really touching the hearts of those of us who so hungrily listen."[1] Not to speak from the heart is not fully to engage the mind either. To speak to the depth of the whole person both the head and the heart must be addressed meaningfully, and not separately. In *Ranald Bannerman's Boyhood*, George

13

MacDonald describes the importance of the heart in such matters. He writes:

> It is not necessary that the intellect should define and separate before the heart and soul derive nourishment. As well say that a bee can get nothing out of a flower, because she does not understand botany. . . . The best influences which bear upon us are of this vague sort—powerful upon the heart and conscience, although undefined to the intellect.[2]

I begin by placing emphasis on the heart because the theological training of most American preachers has already had an ample dose of emphasis placed on the mind—and rightly so. As Soren Kierkegaard once observed, we do not receive nourishment simply by chewing, but by chewing food. There is a necessary and important place for the work of the mind in preparation for the delivery of Christian sermons. But this ought not be done at the expense of the heart—either the preacher's heart or the hearts of the preacher's listeners. My aim in this book is to strike a balance between these two, the head and the heart, and to encourage preaching that addresses them both in thoughtful and helpful ways.

Chapter 1 introduces the importance of the head and heart connection and discusses ways of knowing and of telling the Christian story. It concludes with a discussion of preaching as science, art, or craft. Chapter 2 discusses the importance of the preacher as the person in the pulpit and develops the themes of integrity, authenticity, and authority in defining the character of that person. Chapter 3 turns its attention to the listener and discusses ways of valuing the listener in the preparation and delivery of sermons. Chapter 4 focuses on how to develop an effective head and heart connection in preaching under the themes of silence, method, movement, and metaphor. Chapter 5 develops several practical principles for more effectively communicating the head and heart connection. Included among these principles are partnering, action, freeing the text, listening, speaking, and scripting. Chapter 6 presents two sermons that attempt to make the head and heart connection effectively as examples of some of the themes developed in the book. A postscript, The Preacher's Kitchen Work, is a final reminder of the hard work and the importance of the task that is before all of us preachers: the faithful weekly proclamation of the gospel of Jesus Christ through the instrumentality of our own hearts and minds.

Realizing that both women and men are called to the weekly preaching office, I've chosen to handle the awkward "he/she" pronoun dilemma by alternating usage with each chapter.

When Evelyn Underhill was an already recognized scholar in Christian mysticism, she sought out Baron von Hügel as her spiritual guide. He, in turn, told her that first she would need to go and spend two afternoons a week in the ghetto. This was necessary, he explained to her, because "If properly entered into and persevered with it will discipline, mortify, deepen, and quiet you. It will, as it were, distribute your blood—some of your blood—away from your brain, where too much is lodged at present."[3] The movement of some of our own preacher's blood—not all of it but some of it from our heads to our hearts is important for us too if we intend to speak as faithfully and well as we can from our own hearts and minds to the hearts and minds of our listeners.

A well-known Chinese proverb counsels that a journey of a thousand miles begins with the first step. In a more prosaic manner, Captain Woodrow Call, in Larry McMurtry's Pulitzer Prize–winning novel *Lonesome Dove,* says to his partner, Augustus McCrae, and the other cowboys preparing for the long cattle drive from Texas to Montana, "Well, I reckon it's time to go . . . We'll never get there if we don't start."[4]

Yes, indeed. And so now, as Captain Call might have put it, we commence getting started. I am glad to have your company.

**Thomas R. Swears**
Wilmington, Delaware

# 1

# THE IMPORTANCE OF THE HEAD AND HEART CONNECTION

☙

Doctrine taught does not penetrate the minds of the needy, if a compassionate heart does not commend it to the hearts of hearers.

GREGORY THE GREAT
*Pastoral Care*

## The Journey Begins

The longest journey anyone ever takes doesn't require a single step. It is an internal journey from the head to the heart. Although anatomically it is a distance of but a few inches, spiritually it takes a lifetime to complete. It is life's central journey and without attempting it life always will be less than it could be. Writing in *Humboldt's Gift* Saul Bellow says of it: "By themselves abstractions will not travel. They must pass through the

17

heart to be transmitted."[1] This is true both of living one's own life fully and of proclaiming the gospel effectively to others. Christian preaching often does one thing at the expense of another. It addresses the head but doesn't touch the heart. Or, it moves the heart without challenging the mind. Either way, it is less than it could be because it is not addressing the whole person. It is when both the head and the heart are addressed that the volition of the hearer can be engaged and a meaningful response evoked. And the evoking of such a response is much more likely to happen when the whole being of the listener is addressed. Speaking to the mind only allows the listener to maintain distance, speculating, rationalizing, critiquing rather than being engaged. Speaking to the heart only allows the listener so to individuate and spiritualize the message as to need only to experience it in the moment rather than to be further compelled to respond to it concretely in the actual life of responsible discipleship in the world. It is, rather, the intentional connection of head and heart in preaching that is the most compelling, evoking responses from both the preacher and the listener.

I once heard Gardner Taylor, who was for several decades the powerful and passionate preacher of the Concord Baptist Church in Brooklyn, tell of strolling in the old chapel at Harvard when he came upon a plaque with a line from Ralph Waldo Emerson on it that read, "Acquaint thyself with deity." Taylor said that such instruction awed him, as it should any preacher with half a heart and an ounce of sense. "Acquaint thyself with deity," it said; not "acquaint thy mind," or "acquaint thy heart," or "acquaint thy spirit," but "acquaint thyself," that is, the whole self—body, mind, heart, memory, will, spirit, soul. Apply your whole being to the worship of God and to the honoring of God's presence in you through the conduct of your life.

Words are the most important and sacred tools available to preachers for the accomplishment of this task. It is vitally important, both in preaching and in pastoral care, never to underestimate them. In the Bible, as in life, words are used to bless and to condemn, to wound and to heal, to delineate and to deceive, to loosen and to bind. They are deeds and they change lives. If words have no effect then how else, in this century alone, do we explain the powerful influence of Adolph Hitler, FDR, Winston Churchill, or John F. Kennedy?

No, words are deeds, and they do, in fact, change lives. Think, for instance, of the first time you heard just these three simple one syllable words, "I love you," spoken to you by someone you cared deeply about. Or imagine other simple words being spoken to you by someone you have cared deeply about for a long time and still do: "I don't love you anymore." How safe are simple words such as those? How powerful? How wounding? It simply isn't true that "sticks and stones can break my bones but words can never hurt me." Yes, they can; and often they do. Some of the deepest hurt and the deepest joy both preacher and listener will ever know is experienced in the form of the spoken word and is rooted in its power to evoke response.

No one knew and respected the power of words more than Jesus did. In Matthew he says this clearly: "I tell you, on the day of judgment you will have to give an account for every careless word you utter; for by your words you will be justified, and by your words you will be condemned" (Matthew 12:36-37). Jesus knew that the fundamental human sacrament is speech. It is the way we bless and the way we curse both those we don't know and those we know the best and both love and hurt the most deeply.

Words are the tools of the preacher's trade and the pastor's counsel. Preachers often intuitively know something of the power of their words and so resist doing their best in the pulpit not because they fear their preaching has no power, but because they fear that it does. And not many preachers really want to be partner to the disquieting of another's soul, to the person who comes up after church and says, "Preacher, I heard what you said today and I believe it. I need to talk with you right away. My life is on the line." The seventeenth-century divine Richard Baxter understood this power and need very well when he said that he preached as a dying man to dying men.

Fred B. Craddock, who, along with Gardner Taylor, was named in a Baylor University survey as one of the ten greatest preachers speaking in the English language today, says that there are two kinds of preaching people won't listen to: bad preaching and good preaching. Bad preaching is resisted because it is an irritation and an insult. Good preaching is resisted because it both requires too much of the listener and reveals too much of the listener to himself. Yet, preaching that does not so require and so reveal is always less than it can be. Augustine perhaps had something like this in mind when he observed that those who stand near the Christ stand near the fire. It is not, and ought not be, comfortable to stand in the clarifying presence of holiness. As George MacDonald once observed, nothing is as deadening to a sense of divine urging as is the habitual dealing with the outside of holy things. Preaching that does not address the whole person may be comfortable to listen to. It may even be stimulating and engaging. But it will lack any essential power to effect an authentic inner response—what the Quakers refer to as "the inner rising"—of the listener. Preaching that touches the mind alone has no soul, no passion. Preaching that touches the heart alone has no weight, no substance. Preaching that touches the mind and the heart forms the soul, the substantive inner life of the believer. The longest journey either preachers or listeners ever take is a journey of but a few inches—from the head to the heart. It is a difficult journey to undertake, but in undertaking it both preacher and listener begin to honor more deeply the presence of Christ in them. Neither scholarship nor faith that does not also touch holiness will ever be all it is capable of becoming either in itself or in the nurture of others.

## The Starting Place

This then is where we begin, at the place where the church gathers Sunday after Sunday, week after week, year after year, longing for a good word—a word of guidance, a word of hope, a word of conviction, a word of wonder, a word of encouragement, a word of healing to be spoken. And it is the preacher's high honor and singular responsibility to speak that word faithfully, compassionately and clearly.

In an earlier time this task was so highly valued that James Stalker said of it:

> I like to think of the minister as only one of the congregation set apart by the rest for a particular purpose. They say to him: Look, brother, we are busy with our daily toils, and confused with cares, but we eagerly long for peace and light to illuminate our life, and we have heard there is a land where these are to be found, a land of repose and joy, full of thoughts that breathe and words that burn, but we cannot go thither ourselves.

**21**

> We are too embroiled in daily cares. Come, we will
> elect you, and set you free from toil, and you shall go
> thither for us and week by week trade with that land
> and bring us its treasures and its spoils.[2]

The task of preaching can become so highly cher-
ished and effective once again when the heart and the
mind of the preacher speak with clarity and compassion to the heart and the mind of the listener, thereby
evoking from the listener not admiration for the
preacher's faith or skill but the response of the listener's
whole being, both head and heart, to the gospel. The
key to releasing the power and grace present in such
proclamation as that lies in the head and heart being
connected in response, evoking not necessarily what the
preacher anticipates but what the Holy Spirit nurtures
or compels. The capacity for such preaching could be
strengthened in the preacher by an awareness of and a
respect for the ebb and flow of the richness of faith and
doubt, joy and sorrow, conviction and vacillation,
strength and weakness, clarity and confusion in the
lives of the listeners present in the sanctuary on a given
Sunday, were the inner content of those lives to be honestly reported.

Preaching doesn't actually occur in a pristine, ideal,
safe, and well-ordered environment, although that is
just what the sanctuary appears to be on Sunday morning. The flowers are in place, the paraments are set,
hymnals and greeter cards are in order, fresh bulletins
are ready for distribution with attentive ushers ready
to do the distributing, and the sound of the choir is
faintly heard down the hallway as it rehearses the
anthem one final time. No, to the discerning inner eye
the sanctuary is actually at the vortex of the human
drama of the lives of those who are gathering there,
seeking something they couldn't name but long for or

else they wouldn't be there. It is this unnamed longing deeper than words that Christian preaching at its best addresses. It does so, often perhaps, only in a slanted, indirect way. But at least in attempting to do so it acknowledges and honors the unarticulated longing of hearts and minds that fills the sanctuary. If that longing is not in some way named or pointed to, then no matter how eloquent or impressive the speech and demeanor of the preacher might be that day, the people are left with their spiritual hunger unfilled and their inarticulate longing unaddressed. And now perhaps added to that hunger and longing is guilt and a sense of inadequacy that their own faith, their own life's journey, when compared with that of the preacher, seems so fragile, so slight. However, the goal of Christian preaching is not the admiration of the preacher but the proclamation of the gospel and the encouragement and guidance of the people with the word and promise of God. This is best done when both the minds and the hearts of those who preach and of those who listen are engaged in the act of preaching, evoking from them holistic responses to the word that is spoken and the word that is heard. How best to speak that word so that it is both heard and felt is the central task this book addresses.

The journey is begun with a prayer I have written and use daily. It is placed here with the hope that it may in some way also offer encouragement to the reader as we set out to undertake the longest journey together. As a result of our journey may those who listen to our preaching also find encouragement and courage to undertake their own.

I offer to you now, O Lord
the chalice which is the life

you have given to me.
I ask you of your grace and mercy
to cleanse and purify me,
to heal me,
to re-form me,
and then to fill me once again
with precious, fresh new wine
of your kingdom
for the living of this day's life.
In Jesus' name. Amen.

# Ways of Knowing

Here are two basic ways of "knowing" whether or not something is true: "Oh, I don't know. My heart just tells me it's right, that's all" and "You'd better think it over carefully. Better safe than sorry, you know." The heart and the mind each decide certain matters in life, and for most of us one or the other generally dominates to a degree. This difference is discerned by one of the sets of preferences measured by the Keirsey Temperament Sorter.[3] One of the preferences measured by this scale is that of the choices made between intuition and cognition when attempting to order one's world. According to Carl Jung's theory of personality, on which the Keirsey Temperament Sorter is based, no one is ever wholly one way or the other. Rather each person is somewhere on a continuum, at times favoring intuition and at other times favoring reason when ordering the world and arriving at decisions. All normally psychologically healthy persons use both feeling and thinking when processing information, but to differing degrees.

This information can also be helpful to preachers, a part of whose central weekly task is to elicit a response from those who attend to their preaching. Knowing that those listeners will use both their hearts and their minds in forming that response can serve as an encouragement to the preacher to address both the heart and the mind in the sermon so as to engage the whole person's response. Ideally what is being sought is a balance between intellect and emotion that can speak a clear gospel word both to the mind and to the heart. When this is effectively done then preaching can be clear, moving, powerful, and unmanipulative because it is then neither a matter solely of cerebral address nor solely of the titillation of the heart strings, but an authentic word of address to the whole person—body, heart, mind, and soul.

Edward Farley, retired professor of theology at Vanderbilt University Divinity School and author of *The Fragility of Knowledge,* was once asked if he thought that theological education focused too much "on the cognitive dimension of learning as opposed to personal and social transformation," that is, to doing and feeling. He responded, in part, that "genuine knowing is always driven by a passion" and that "without a passion we won't submit ourselves to what it takes to really know something." This passion for knowing more holistically is what Plato called *eros.* Most people's fullest way of knowing is already oriented by such a passion about something, and that passion is already a matter of flesh and blood, of both their hearts and their minds.[4] The preacher's task then is not to create such a reality but to recognize it, to value it, and to respond to it out of the inner language of the preacher's own heart and mind. Preaching to the heart and to the mind is not an attempt to create a new language but rather an attempt to speak once again our most ancient and basic human language, the one that is understood by the heart and the mind at the same time. It is not an easy language to master, but its rewards can be deeply affecting. It is the language more of Jesus than of Paul, more of Kierkegaard than of Barth, more of the story-teller than of the reporter. It is the language that speaks to the heart and that the mind comprehends, that speaks to the mind and that the heart nurtures. For preachers it is, in other words, the sweetly compelling, starkly demanding language of the gospel of Jesus Christ, which requires much more than the tongue to be spoken faithfully and well; it requires also the heart and the mind and the soul of the speaker.

Our minds can teach us many things; some things, however, are truly known only to the heart. Beauty is one such thing. Love is another, as is grace. Our minds can learn and remember how far it is to the moon but only our hearts can teach us why anyone would ever want to go there. It is only when both the heart and the mind are meaningfully addressed that the inner journey covering the vast distance between them is effectively begun.

The writer George Tyrrell, commenting on this mind and heart connection, said of it,

> Let us not then imagine that we have finished our duty by swallowing revelation wholesale in submission to external authority; we swallow that we may digest, and we digest that we may live the eternal life of the mind and heart by an intelligent sympathy with the mind and heart of God.[5]

Such an intelligent sympathy with the mind and heart of God as well as with the minds and hearts of those who patiently listen to Christian preaching today, waiting and hoping for a good word to be spoken to them, is a principal goal of preaching to both the heart and the mind, that is, so that a good word might be formed, spoken, heard, understood, felt, and responded to.

## Ways of Telling

Earlier this century a great debate took place between Rudolph Bultmann and C. S. Dodd concerning the nature of the gospel. Bultmann said that the gospel was a word of direct address challenging the volition and demanding a response from the listener. Dodd said the gospel was a narrative word, telling a story, evoking a response from the listener through the listener's identification with the story rather than demanding a response based on direct discourse. Their debate was a healthy and necessary one, and both of them were right. There is both direct discourse and narrative form in the gospels, even within the teaching of Jesus himself.

No one way of preaching needs to dominate in order for the preacher to be effective. In fact, there is truth in the opposite view, that is, that using different preaching styles for different literary forms of biblical text is the most effective model to follow because it provides for integrity of form between text and sermon. As some seasoned elder preachers might put it, speaking of such matters, "You can't win all the races with the same horse." The narrative sermon is not the only form that can address both the mind and the heart. In fact the use of narrative style is no guarantee of this at all. Inappropriate, disconnected, or fluffy stories address neither the mind nor the heart to any positive effect. On the other hand, a thoughtful expository sermon can address both of them quite well. It is not the form that makes the difference; it is the aware-

27

ness, intentionality, integrity, and skill of the preacher that does so.

Perhaps a brief review of some of today's more common preaching settings will help place this discussion in a broader context. The first of these settings is that of the Holiness, Pentecostal, and Charismatic traditions. In this style a strong emphasis is placed upon feeling and experience as the listener's response to the sermon. The emphasis is primarily on the heart. As a young man I once attended a large Assembly of God revival at Cobo Hall in Detroit. The hymns, soloists, warm-up speakers, and carefully modulated music all built toward a fevered pitch as the featured preacher took the podium. The entire event was focused on the heart's conversion in an auditorium filled with perhaps a thousand or more already converted hearts. Minds there had little to do because hearts were so filled to overflowing.

A second common setting for preaching is that of liturgical worship, where consistent order and carefully crafted language and musical settings are a strong focal point. Episcopal, Lutheran, and Roman Catholic churches are primary representations of this tradition. I remember being surprised as a young boy in the 1950s when I once attended a Roman Catholic mass with a cousin of mine and no sermon was preached at all. I later attended an Episcopal funeral service and no sermon was preached there either. This seemed like quite an advantage to a Lutheran boy who regularly had to endure forty-minute Sunday sermons and more than a few such funeral sermons as well. Today's liturgical churches are rediscovering an emphasis on preaching, but the liturgy is still central to their sense of worship.

A third common setting for preaching is that of the

straight expository sermon delivered from a central pulpit, often dominating over a much smaller communion table located beneath it. This setting is common to churches of the Reformed tradition where the sermon is the central event in the worship service. Historically the emphasis here has been on thought and reason, with little adornment. I once visited John Calvin's church in Geneva and saw that the only noticeable liturgical accoutrements in that rather large nave were the simple chair Calvin sat in, the Bible he read from, and the pulpit from which he preached. I grew up in a Lutheran version of this tradition where for the first eighteen years of my life I thought verse-by-verse expository preaching was the only kind of preaching there was. From the particular version of it I heard, I concluded that my salvation was not so much a matter of grace and faith as it was of proper information. Where is Mount Ararat after all? Was Jericho south or west of Jerusalem? And how far? This sort of thing is what I got out of most of it.

It took me years to realize that information alone is not salvific, that it is the gospel that is salvific. And when I finally did realize it, it was because the gospel was addressed both to my mind and to my heart. My passion now is to encourage preachers so to preach that their listeners may both hear and feel and thus know themselves to be wholly addressed by the gospel and thus set free and encouraged to follow Christ faithfully in their own lives.

In order to speak to others in such a way, it is important first to discuss whether our own current sermons are primarily conveyers of information, works of art, or labors of love. It is to that consideration we will now turn our attention.

# Science, Art, or Craft?

If preaching is primarily a science, then thorough hermeneutic and exegetical study alone ought to render a sermon that is accurate, meaningful, and helpful. Yet most Christians have listened to enough such technically correct and accurate sermons and not, in any significant way, been affected by them to know that that simply isn't true. Gardener Taylor once humorously observed, commenting on such sermons, "At least the Lord's people learned patience that day." And Fred Craddock says of such sermons, where "nothin' moves" and "nothin' twitters," that where the response of the people to them is indifference or boredom, such a response is a serious matter because boredom isn't funny, it's demonic. To be bored when addressed by the grace and beauty and power of the gospel is to know that you have not heard a proper presentation of it. There is too much pain and meaninglessness in the lives of the people sitting in Christian sanctuaries week after week to allow such a condition to go unanswered. The cost is simply too high.

Effective Christian preaching is more than the objective presentation of accurate information. Saul Bellow stated the truth about such matters succinctly and well with his earlier noted observation that abstractions do not travel by themselves but must pass through the heart to be transmitted. He was referring to the language of human relationship with that comment, but it can be appropriated for the language of preaching as well. Information alone does not save and rarely moves anyone. There is a truth in the gospel to be spoken and heard that transcends the presentation of information.

Writer and teacher Beldan Lane tells of a time when

he was reading the story of Cinderella to his then young daughter. When he had finished reading she looked up at him and said, "Is it true, Daddy? Did that really happen?" Lane says that fortunately he had enough sense to pause before answering her to consider at what level she was asking the question, because he knew that things can be "true" for us in different ways. If she wanted to know if there had been an actual girl named Cinderella to whom these things had happened, then his answer would have been a carefully worded discussion of the nature and purpose of fairy-tales and myths, appropriate for her level of comprehension. If she were really asking him something about herself, however, his response would have been quite different. If her real question was, "Daddy, can the things that I think are ugly in me be changed? Can I be beautiful some day, too?" then his response would have been, "Yes, baby, the story is true—it is very, very true." His answer would have been not only compassionate but also accurate, because the essence of the tale is about hope and transformation in the face of difficulty. Beldan Lane did not want to be the father who gave his child a stone when she asked for bread, and he wasn't. But, did he deceive her in the process? After all, is the story of Cinderella really *true*? Well, each of us must decide that answer for ourselves. I simply want to point out that all sorts of things are *true* for us in different ways, on different levels, all the time. What, for instance, is love actually? Is it a thought? A feeling? A desire? A deed? A memory? An absence? A presence? An ache? A longing? The answer, of course, is yes to each of these and to more as well. Any definition of love that does not include both the mind and the heart falls far short of a full understanding of the word. There is a truth to be told in the preaching of the gospel that transcends the dissemination of information and reaches out to touch both the hearer's heart and the hearer's mind.

If preaching is primarily an art, then rhetorical, theatrical, and elocutionary skills alone ought to render a sermon meaningful and helpful. Yet thoughtful Christians, even where impressed by such demonstrated skill, know, upon reflection, that many such sermons have lacked substance and depth and often clear purpose as well. They simply do not stand up to the careful scrutiny of actual lived experience. Admiration of the preacher's skill does little to sustain the listener for long.

Preaching as an art places emphasis on performance, on the gifts and skills of the preacher, so that the primary response of the listener is likely to be either the admiration of a generous heart or the envy of a petty one. The preacher as a public artist is admired. The pastor who speaks to the longing heart and inquiring mind of the listener out of a faithful heart and mind of his own is loved. The nineteenth-century writer John Watson wrote of this distinction in a book entitled *The Cure of Souls*. He wrote: "The preacher has admiration for his peculiar reward, but the pastor has affection: if the preacher be ill there are paragraphs in the newspapers; if the pastor, there is concern in humble homes. No [person] in human society gathers such a harvest of kindly feeling as the shepherd of souls, none is held in such grateful memory."[6] Chief among the reasons such a pastor gathers a harvest of kindly feeling is that when he speaks to the people, in their homes, at their sick beds, at the gravesides of their loved ones, or from the pulpit, the words flow from both the mind and the heart of the pastor to the mind and the heart of the listener.

The danger of preaching primarily as an art form is twofold. First, the danger to the preacher is vanity and hubris, a blurring of the gospel's message with one's own self and skills. Second, if admiration of the preacher's performance skills is the primary response of the listener, then nothing much, if anything, of substance is being required from him, which is to say that no meaningful response to the gospel is being evoked by the sermon. Neither of these responses to preaching—vanity or admiration—is spiritually healthy in the long run. Much, much better would be engagement with the sermon on the part of the listener and awe and humility on the part of the preacher that God would use even his words to evoke in the heart and mind of another human being a response, not to the preacher but to the gospel.

If preaching is primarily neither science nor art, primarily neither information nor emotion and admiration, then what is it? And what is there about it, at its best, that informs the mind and forms the heart into the image and likeness of Christ? A good word to describe the potentially powerful yoking of science and art in preaching is the word *craft,* which has an honored history of describing the way in which the labor and skill and knowledge and passion of the craftsman were welded together in the service of their craft, often resulting in an object of beauty, utility, and durability helpful to others for long periods of time.

In this sense preaching too is more a craft then it is either a science or an art. At its best, it touches the depths of the preacher's own heart and mind and yokes them in an intentional, dynamic, substantive way that becomes far more than the attempted wedding of information and emotion. It becomes the deep bonding of heart, mind, memory, volition, and visceral response to the word, which has not simply been spoken accurately and properly but has also been spoken deeply, vitally, authentically, holistically, from the center of one person's soul to the center of another's. Such preaching is powerful and effective not because it is particularly impressive intellectually or admirable artistically but because it has integrity and because it is evocative of that which is identified by the listener to dwell within himself rather than that which is to be admired in the speaker from a distance. In other words, the strength of such preaching is its evocative power. Its strength does not issue from the preacher alone and then get tamped into the listeners. Rather it issues from the dynamic interaction of the spoken and the heard word, from the active engagement of the hearts and the minds of both the one who is speaking and those who are being spoken to.

In summary, preaching as a hermeneutic science emphasizes information and its accurate transmission; preaching as an art emphasizes communication and public speaking skills; preaching as a craft emphasizes the relationship between the craftsman, the tools, the learning of the craft, and the valuing of the apprentice. The communication of the craftsman is at once practical, specific, and relational. Both the craftsman (preacher) and the apprentice (listener) need to be involved concretely with the task if anything of true learning and worth is to issue from it.

The effective preacher is more the skilled craftsman than either the informed scientist or the admired artist, although elements of each of these are part of the preacher's craft. The truly effective pastoral preacher stands neither above people tamping information into them nor at a distance from them, admired but unreachable. Rather such a preacher is one who takes the risks involved in evoking from others what is already in them and then in wonder and humility watches what God can do with it. The *recompense* for such faithful preaching is very great indeed.

# 2

# THE PERSON IN THE PULPIT

## INTEGRITY, AUTHENTICITY, AND AUTHORITY IN PREACHING TO HEAD AND HEART

cJ₽

A minister of Christ should have his tongue, his heart, and his hand agree.

JEROME
*Ad Nepotianum*

## Integrity

Jerome's statement is about congruency in the life of the Christian minister. It is wise counsel as valid and timely today as it was in the fourth century, and contemporary preachers ignore it at their own risk. The Christian pastor is called to be a person of integrity who, in order to be believable and trustworthy in the pulpit, must first be believable and trustworthy, that is, worthy of trust, in daily life. Such a believable and trustworthy person is one in whom there is clear and

37

evident harmony between word and deed. In other words, such a person is a person of integrity, from the Latin *integer*, meaning "sound, whole, entire."

It does not mean this in our modern compulsive sense of perfectionism but rather in the sense of possessing the quality of sound moral principle. To use a single contemporary word to express Jerome's more poetic language: A minister of Christ should be a person of integrity. Who the preacher is, what the preacher says, and what the preacher does all express the same singular reality: the presence of a believable, trustworthy fellow human being whose words in the pulpit are congruent with her actions when out of the pulpit. Such a person is, of course, far from perfect in our modern sense of "without fault or error," but does intentionally attempt to live out the biblical meaning of the word *perfect,* which is more accurately captured by our English word *mature.* The New Testament meaning of the word doesn't share our American obsessiveness over perfectionism. In the biblical sense, rather, the word *perfect* means to make room for growth and for the inevitable disappointments and failures and foibles that are present in any human life fully engaged and honestly reported. This is as true of the preacher as it is of anyone. Integrity for the preacher, then, is not perfection in all behavior but honesty about her behavior and movement toward maturity in Christ. The first necessary act in such movement is the conscious acknowledgment that one needs so to move and to grow. Without such intention, complacency and self-deception can easily replace commitment and honesty, and the movement toward growth and change, that is, toward maturity in Christ and personal integrity, will atrophy. When this occurs perhaps the semblance of integrity will appear in the pulpit, but not its substance.

And at least one person in the sanctuary will know it—the preacher. Concerning such matters, the nineteenth-century writer Johann Michael Sailer penned these words:

> The life of the preacher must be the prologue of the sermon he would preach, the commentary on what he really teaches and the epilogue, the seal of the sermons he has preached. The preacher is not he who teaches for an hour on Sundays and festivals, but he teaches by deeds, for whole weeks, months, years, his whole life long, what he preaches on particular days in words.[1]

And the seventeenth-century divine Richard Baxter said further of it:

> Moreover, take heed to yourselves, lest your example contradict your doctrine, and lest you lay such stumbling blocks before the blind, as may be the occasion of their ruin; lest you may unsay that with your lives, which you say with your tongues; and be the greatest hinderers of the success of your own labors. It much hindereth our work . . . if we contradict ourselves . . . if your actions give your tongue the lie . . . if you build up an hour or two with your mouths, and all the week after pull down with your hands![2]

Baxter's observation is the seventeenth-century version of the ministerial act of shooting oneself in the homiletical foot. People are not stupid. They lack neither power of observation nor insight. And they simply will not place much, if any, credence in a Sunday preacher who lacks in the daily round of life among them what Jerome long centuries ago correctly intuited a minister of Christ must possess: integrity of tongue and heart and hand.

Consider for a moment an understanding of who a

"holy person" is by moving away from an image of someone who is especially pious or nearly perfect in all matters of faith and life toward an understanding of such a person being someone in whose presence you are reminded of the presence of God. Such a presence is not always nor ought it always be comfortable. It ought not be a light, easy thing to stand in the presence of holiness, as Augustine reminds us with his teaching that the one who stands near the Christ stands near the fire. Now, using this sense of a holy person, what qualities does such a person possess that somehow remind you of the presence of God? Comfort? Perhaps, but not necessarily. Wisdom? Compassion? Strength? Peace? Yes, to these, but yes too to guidance, discipline, discernment, discomfort, and judgment as well. What is sensed at the core of such a person's character is integrity—a transparent, consistent, intentional harmony of word and deed. Such a person will not be lightly dismissed by others, because her holiness is not that of perfection but of deeply held gospel passion. What such a person says will be listened to, which is why integrity is of such vital importance in the life of the preacher. The stakes are so high.

## Authenticity

An authentic person is in the category of someone you can easily enough identify but probably can't define. Apparently Emily Dickinson once listened to a sermon delivered by an inauthentic person because she said, in response to the sermon of this visiting preacher: "What confusion would cover the innocent Jesus, to meet so enabled a man!"[3] Her comment helps us see that something other than competence alone is required of preachers who would speak both to the heart and to the mind. There are times, in fact, when a supposed competence, that is, an overwrought, too thorough, too polished, too clear, too neatly wrapped delivered sermon can be a hindrance to effective communication, leaving no gospel word actually spoken, heard, felt, or responded to. This is not to speak against competence and preparation but to speak for authenticity and integrity, which is to emphasize the importance of the person of the preacher in the actual presentation of the sermon.

There simply is no substitute for authentic personhood in the pulpit. The sermon does not stand alone as an objective artifact to be admired, critiqued, responded to, or disregarded on its intellectual, theological, and artistic merit alone. It is indispensably connected to the life, the faith, the doubt, the compassion, the passion, the history of the woman or the man who is preaching it. And as Emily Dickinson correctly intuited the matter, the grace and blessing present in a sermon are not solely the result of competence. They are, first of all, gifts of the Holy Spirit, which are then nurtured by the preacher in the life of prayer and the disciplines of hard work and thoughtful preparation and then, finally and often reluctantly, spoken into the life of the gathered community. Such a preacher as that may well be an "enabled" one, but will surely also be a faithful, authentic one—one I believe even the astute Emily Dickinson could have listened to profitably and gladly, responding not only to enabled competence but also to integrity and authenticity, that is, to the personhood of the preacher.

Authentic preaching, then, requires of the preacher authentic living, which is best accomplished by the preacher's commitment to live intentionally in the presence of Christ. Preaching lacking in such internal focus is, indiscernibly perhaps but consistently, less than it could be. What makes preaching authentic (and sensed to be so by the listeners) is neither the preacher's skill nor the preacher's faith but the presence of Christ discerned by the listeners to be present, active and communicated through that skill and faith to them.

In all of this there needs to be an openness to mystery, to humility, and to humor in the preacher. This is so because the task of preaching is not the neat unassailable provision of answers to compliant, unquestioning listeners but, at its truest and best, the opening of the hearts and minds and volitions of those listeners to form their own responses to the word that has been spoken. There is both danger and possibility in such an approach. The danger is that the listeners may form responses perceived to be incorrect or inappropriate, even heretical, by the preacher. At times, such an approach also can lead listeners to place credit or lay blame at the feet of the preacher for things she never said. This can be either blessing or bane depending, of course, on just what it is the preacher is being credited with or blamed for. The possibility exists that the listeners may just form a response not conceived by and thus also not limited to the preacher's thought and vision. Such a response may well be richer, fuller, deeper, more thoughtful and substantive than that of the preacher, which from the vain preacher's perspective could be threatening and disconcerting but to the authentic preacher's heart can be a great, if mysterious and humbling, satisfaction and joy, because such a preacher also knows of yet another possibility: possibly, just possibly, the listener's responses have been Spirit-led.

To some existentialist philosophers *authenticity* denotes a way of existing in which a person has become genuinely herself without pretense. The German equivalent for this is *eigentlichkeit,* from the word *eigen,* meaning "own." So to be authentic is to be one's own and truest self. Yet because no human existence can be truly authentic without a communal dimension, there can be no authenticity in Christian community without mutual respect and love. The preacher who is unwilling to learn from her listeners the truth she has to tell has not yet fully learned to be her own truest, most authentic self regarding both herself and them.

A thorough analysis by Hans van der Geest of some two hundred worship services and sermons revealed three strong desires on the part of those who regularly listen to Christian preaching. The strongest desire was that the worship service and the sermon be personal. The second desire was that the sermon offer release from pressure or tension. The third desire was that the sermon provide some insight "into the existential problems of their lives." These three desires can be summarized as security, deliverance, and understanding. The study further revealed that the content of the sermon is less important than the person of the preacher in engaging the listener. Van der Geest describes it this way: "The content of the words spoken is not an unimportant element in the occurrence of this feeling of security, but neither is it the only element, and often not even the most important. The more deeply the listeners feel themselves engaged and spoken to, the more security they experience in the service."[4] Van der Geest's research shows that people participating in a worship service clearly desire and expect to be spoken to by the preacher on a deep and meaningful level of experience. The preacher who has not yet learned to be her own most authentic self will find it difficult to speak at such a deep and meaningful level of experience, being already too preoccupied, self-absorbed, and anxious about others' responses to her to be truly present to them and their yearnings for security, deliverance, and understanding.

The preacher can best respond to these deep yearnings by responding to the whole being of the listeners, by speaking not only to the intellectual capacity of their minds but to their heart's memory and their soul's longing as well. It is not only the mind that responds to effective preaching but the heart, the spirit, the memory, the body, the soul, and the will as well.

Effective proclamation of the gospel requires authentic personal witness, and in the sermon the preacher is that witness. The listener's experience of that witness comes through what can, in one sense, be understood as the preacher's presence as a sacramental presence. In the preaching context, the preacher is a concrete physical expression of the grace and blessing of God. Now that is a high and perhaps uncomfortable view of the preaching office, but it is also one that deserves the preacher's careful thought and attention because it is the way in which many of those who weekly attend to the preacher's sermons view the matter.

First Peter 2:5 instructs us that all followers of Christ are called to be a holy priesthood, to become what is commonly called "the priesthood of all believers." Each Christian is to live so as to make evident the mercy and grace of God at work in and through them. As Kathleen Norris has put it, "It's a tall order, to literally *be* a sacrament, and it helps to remember Jesus' statement in the fifteenth chapter of John's Gospel: 'You did not choose me; I chose you.' "[5] In Martin Luther's definition three things are required to make something a sacrament. These three things are that there be a clear command from Christ concerning it (e.g., "Do this in remembrance of me"); that common earthly elements be used (e.g., bread and wine); and that a promise of forgiveness and grace be clearly present (e.g., ". . . shed for you and for all people for the forgiveness of sin"). Arguably the command for preaching can be heard in the echo of the Great Commission ("Go therefore and make disciples . . . teaching them . . ."). The earthly element is the physical being of the preacher, and the promise of grace and forgiveness is the core content of faithful kerygmatic gospel preaching.

My argument here is not for the creation of a new sacrament but rather for moving preachers to a more thoughtful, intentional consideration of the centrality of the preaching office in the exercise of authentic, faithful, gospel-centered pastoral care. Christianity is, after all, an incarnational religion in which the manifestation of Christ's presence among his people is certainly to be no less evident in the life of the preacher than it is in the lives of those to whom she preaches.

One practical implication that develops naturally from this understanding of preaching as a concrete incarnational act of witness is the use of the personal pronoun *I* instead of the more generalized and often unctuous *one*. This difference can be easily sensed in the following two statements: "I believe that Christ will come again soon." and "One has a tendency to think, given certain signs, that perhaps Christ may just possibly return soon." The first statement is one of personal faith and clear disclosure. No one is left to wonder what the preacher thinks about this particular matter. The second statement is so equivocating and generalized as to lose all expression of authenticity in its various hesitancies and qualifications. Who, after all, is this "one" if not the preacher? Then why not say so? What exactly are these *certain signs*? And what in the world does "Christ may just possibly return soon" mean? Will he or won't he? What does the preacher actually think? No one can tell much at all about it from the second statement, except to conclude that the preacher is quite a cautious person, not wanting to reveal too much in case he might offend or she might cause someone else's point of view to be shaken a bit. A simple Zen saying seems fitting here: "Sit, walk, or run, but don't wobble."

In cases such as these we preachers often give ourselves more credit than we deserve. Most people can handle our "deep" thoughts and "innovative" ideas, and frankly, many of them are way ahead of us before we ever open our mouths to speak. The preaching office bestows on preachers no special degree of piety, faith, insight, or intelligence. Many of the people who listen regularly (and patiently) to sermons are more devout, faithful, loving, and intelligent than are we preachers who deliver those sermons. We hold our office by virtue of call, certification, and training, not by virtue of superior moral fiber, faith, or mental acumen. I, for one, regularly preach to people who outdistance me in intelligence, faith, and devotion. At least, then, I can try to be authentically present, honest, and clear with them when I do preach. Ordination to word and sacrament ministry bestows on us preachers superiority in nothing, only rather a deep internal commitment to something: to the faithful pastoral care of God's people given into our charge and to living our own lives intentionally in the presence of Christ and, insofar as we are able, bringing that presence no dishonor through our conduct.

If we preachers worry overmuch about offending or harming, we will never be free to speak the truth we uniquely have been given to speak. The Holy Spirit is quite capable of using our sermons as the Spirit wills. If, by caution and careful calculation, we preachers are less clear than we know we can be, then we ought to be neither surprised nor injured when we overhear some-one saying after church, "Well, the preacher just didn't speak to me today," because in point of fact, we won't have done so. A sermon addressed to the generic "everyman" effectively speaks to no actual man or woman at all. "Everyman" doesn't attend worship, only individual men and women do. It is they who deserve and long to be addressed not by a "one" but by an "I" whom they know and with whom they can agree or disagree without fear of reprisal or put-down. When the sermon is finished they ought at least know they have been taken seriously and spoken to by an actual flesh-and-blood fellow human being. Any normally functioning Christian man or woman with blood puls-ing through his or her veins and a heart beating in his or her chest longs to be addressed on Sunday morning not by a cautious, unctuous, tentative "one" but by a clear and present "I." Even when what "one" says in a sermon is insightful and objectively correct, it only has power for the listener if it's a personal possession of the preacher. If it is sensed by the listener to be an abstrac-tion also for the preacher, it will be received and responded to as such: a vaguely interesting idea but lacking any real substance insofar as one's own actual self is concerned. When the people are in need of a road map and the preacher instead pulls a globe out of the pulpit and starts talking, the people, rightly, stop listen-ing. "One" speaking *about life in general* and *death in general* is a far cry removed from the actual human need that is seated right then and there, in a hundred or more different forms, before the pulpit. Authentic, compassionate pastoral care and fellow human feeling compels the preacher who realizes this to speak to her listeners not as "one" but as "I."

Preachers also can expect their sermons to have positive, meaningful effect only when they first find access to their own experience. This does not mean that the preacher needs to become an emotional exhibitionist in the pulpit. To the contrary, as evidenced by episodes in the lives of television evangelists Jim and Tammy Faye Bakker and Jimmy Swaggart, emotion before one's listeners is no guarantee of emotional or spiritual health, honesty, or authenticity. The opposite of these qualities can easily enough become the actual point in fact, often sustained in the preacher by a delusional self-deception mimicking authentic emotion that becomes a caricature of a spiritually healthy life and appropriate self-disclosure.

Inappropriate emotional and spiritual exhibitionism in the pulpit is a perversion of authenticity. Preachers can become too personal if they tell things about themselves that are thinly veiled expressions of self-congratulations or reaches for compliment, as in "Friends, if I seem a bit off my mark today it's because I was called to the hospital at 4:00 A.M. this morning." Other inappropriate, unnecessary self-disclosures attempting to make oneself "just one of you"—such as "when I think back to my college days and remember the number of co-eds I took sexual advantage of, I really feel bad"—also can have an embarrassing or discomforting effect on the listeners. Even if true such disclosure is unwarranted and unnecessary. There is a limit beyond which something is too personal and too private to be brought into the pulpit. A statement at the beginning of the sermon such as "Friends, I'm actually very tired today and would really rather not be here" is altogether unfitting, even if factual. And if it is actually true then the preacher might do better to provide for someone else to speak that day or, as Jesus counseled Peter about girding himself, do the task as faithfully and well as it can be done without fanfare or sympathy-seeking. Concern for the preacher's energy level, mental health, or sexual history is not what brought the people to church and ought never be the focal point of worship. Rather, Christ is the focal point of worship and the preacher is Christ's steward. If sound stewardship of worship cannot be rendered, then the steward needs a rest and would be well-advised to take it in order to discern the source of the weariness or the need for acclamation before bitterness overtakes faithfulness in the preaching office and tedium replaces joy, because when this happens there are losers: the preacher and the people.

Authentic communication from the pulpit always exists in the tension between disclosure and distance. Because of this tension even seemingly positive qualities such as genuineness and sincerity have their limits. Preachers who disregard proper distance will meet appropriate resistance, even rejection, from their listeners. Two guidelines can help preachers determine to what extent it is appropriate to speak about their own lives and concerns from the pulpit: (1) What is the relevance of this problem or experience for the listeners? and (2) To what extent does this particular problem or experience describe one that is experienced by most people (e.g., sickness, confusion, anger, joy, loss, failure), and thus identifiable to them, rather than one unique to the preacher's own experience?

Because the man or woman doing the preaching is an actual flesh-and-blood being, there is no escaping personal effect in the pulpit, nor ought there be. That effect, however, can be either positive or negative. I don't add the category "neutral" because I consider it to be in the negative category, considering how important preaching is to the life and spiritual health of those

**49**

who hear it. Authenticity can be present in the pulpit only when it is also experienced by others as present outside of the pulpit. The preacher whose demeanor and behavior is pastoral and compassionate in the pulpit but small and petty outside of it is not someone of whom the word *authentic* is an apt description. The word *duplicitous,* from the Latin *duplicitas,* meaning "doubleness," conveys a more telling and likely more accurate description. I don't know anyone who would knowingly suffer a duplicitous person gladly outside of the pulpit, so why in the world would they want to do so with someone who is in it?

In the final analysis it is really a matter of character and a question of whether or not we preachers are willing to make ourselves clearly understandable, and thus also vulnerable to our listeners. Preaching is a costly business, or it ought to be. Some soul-searching is in order for preachers to whom it comes too easily, who carry it too lightly as an adornment, who are a bit too eager to mount the pulpit steps. Soren Kierkegaard was asked once why he regularly attended worship at a small dark chapel where attendance was sparse and the music modest while thousands each Sunday were attending the impressive, uplifting preaching services of Copenhagen's leading pulpiteer of the day. He replied that he went to worship where he heard Christ crucified preached by someone who knew Christ and loved him, and that that was perhaps why so few gathered there on a Sunday morning.

Authentic Christian preaching is that which is done faithfully and consistently, week after week, month after month, season after season, year after year, by women and men whose words are congruous with their actions whether they are in the pulpit, at the office, on the phone, at the hospital, at the grocery store, among friends, or in their own homes—especially in their own homes.

## Authority

Matthew concludes his description of the Sermon on the Mount with this observation: "Now when Jesus had finished saying these things, the crowds were astounded at his teaching, for he taught them as one having authority, and not as their scribes" (Matthew 7:28-29). Men and women who are preaching as we now end the tumultuous twentieth century are some considerable distance removed from this awe-filled response to Jesus' preaching, just as we are also removed from the response of the people to the early Puritan preachers like Cotton Mather and Jonathan Edwards, whose sermons were the voice of authority in colonial New England. What then is the nature of our own authority in the preaching office today?

Max Weber's classic distinction between power and authority provides a good starting point. Weber describes power as coercive and authority as requiring the consent of those over whom it is exercised. Authority then is the capacity to have one's advice and insight taken seriously. Power, in contrast, is the capacity to decide what happens.[6] Given these definitions, preaching is much more about exercising authority than about exercising power. And the exercising of such authority in the pastoral ministry today is a complex mixture of ecclesiastical, charismatic, personal, and democratic ingredients. It is ecclesiastical by reason of ordination. It is charismatic by reason of call. It is personal by reason of talent, skill, and education. And it is democratic by reason of the willingness of the listeners to give their attention to it. Pastoral authority also has a paradoxical nature in that the one whom God has called to be a servant is also to be a leader among the people she is called to serve, so that the denial or abdication of this leadership role is a contradiction of the call to ministry that has been validated by the church through ordination.[7]

An important aspect of the pastor's authority is the congregation's tacit agreement that the pastor has earned the right to lead by virtue of either religious authenticity or demonstrated competence or both. Yet, as many seasoned pastors now know, the congregation's initial tacit agreement concerning the pastor's assumed abilities must be proven in actual practice in the daily life of the congregation. New pastors often experience this congregational dynamic as a sort of "second ordination," the one in which the parishioners actually accept the pastor's legitimacy to lead. In other words, the pastor's authority has a key relational dimension associated with it. Pastors don't possess authority apart from a community that entrusts them with it.[8] And it is this trust which becomes the foundation on which effective head and heart communication can be established between the pastor and the people both from the pulpit and in their daily life together in Christ.

One expression of this authority that is especially important for pastors to be mindful of, particularly in understanding the head and heart connection between themselves and the people they serve, is their authority as representations of the sacred. Whether they like it or not preachers are the institutionalized representatives of the sacred in society, and no amount of denial or "Oh, gosh, not me" humility about it will change that fact. The wiser course for the pastor is to understand this dynamic more deeply, rather than deny it or humor it, so as to become a more, not less, effective head and heart communicator with those entrusted by God to her spiritual care.

In describing the catholic version of pastoral authority, Urban Holmes calls the priest a *theotokos,* that is, a "God-bearer" or a "mystagogue."[9] To be such a person is to lead others more deeply into the mystery and pathos that surrounds life. The importance of the role of the priest is not in the priest's piety or moral character but in the priest's status as a bearer of the sacred in the midst of the community. For the preacher to understand this is also for her to come closer to speaking to both the hearts and the minds of her listeners.

In contrast to the *theotokos* understanding of pastoral authority is the evangelical or pietistic view, which places greater emphasis precisely on the moral character and personal piety of the one to whom that authority is being entrusted. At the core of this understanding of a pastor's authority to lead and to preach is the high value placed by the people upon that person's inward call from God.[10] Here also a sound understanding of the importance the people place upon the preacher's inner sense of call can become a strong ally in helping the pastor speak effectively both to the hearts and to the minds of her listeners.

In either of these views of pastoral authority there is the perception on the part of the people that the ordained minister has a special relationship with God and is God's representative in that community, an instrument of God at work there through which Christ is himself at work.

This understanding of the authority of the ordained minister as either *theotokos* or inwardly called servant is central to the degree of trust the people are willing to place in the ordained minister and so also central to the degree of trust they are willing to invest in that particular person's preaching. Being perceived as a representative of the sacred in the midst of the community of the faithful is in itself a sacred trust as well as one of the most important bases of the local pastor's authority to preach the gospel among those people who, in large measure, have entrusted the care of their souls and their lives in Christ to her ministry.

Yet these same people also can have profoundly ambivalent feelings about this one in whom they have placed great trust. Qualities of resistance can exist alongside qualities of acceptance, qualities of resentment alongside qualities of admiration. Most psychologically healthy people don't want to be unduly dependent on someone else. Even when that dependency possesses certain appealing qualities it is resisted. Thus there can be simultaneously both resentment and unrealistic expectations even of a much loved and admired pastor. Take, for instance, the incident of the woman who approached her pastor in a state of high agitation following a Sunday morning service. With tears in her eyes and irritation in her voice she said to him, "How could you?" and then walked quickly away obviously angry, puzzled, and hurt. This, the pastor was later to learn, was the woman's response to his announcement to the congregation that morning that his wife was pregnant and they were expecting their first baby. A pastor who had sexual relations with his spouse was not part of this woman's view of his proper role.

Given the reality and intensity of reactions such as these, it is understandable that pastors often don't want to be authority figures, not really. What makes the situation even more difficult and complex is that much of this ambivalence about the authority of the pastor occurs at least partially and often nearly entirely on an unconscious level in both the preacher and the people.[11] And this, in turn, is one of the unspoken internal dynamics at work that greets the very first word of every sermon. The sanctuary is alive with expectation but very little of it is discerned. It just is. And because it is there both danger and power are there too. It is little wonder that the wise preacher approaches the pulpit with prudent fear and caution. It really isn't a safe place to be. It's a revealing, discomforting, exhilarating, sobering place to be, a place the gravity of which the seventeenth-century divine Richard Baxter understood when he said that he preached from it, as we've noted earlier, as a dying man to dying men.

Herman Melville apparently also appreciated both the exhilaration and the danger of preaching quite well, as this passage from *Moby Dick* shows:

> The pulpit is ever this earth's foremost part; all the rest comes in its rear; the pulpit leads the world. From thence it is that the storm of God's quick wrath is first descried, and the bow must bear the earliest brunt. From thence it is that the God of breezes fair or foul is first invoked for favorable winds. Yes, the world's a ship on its passage out, and not a voyage complete; and the pulpit is its prow.[12]

The pulpit as the prow of the world's ship on its journey out is both a wonderful and a disturbing image. The prow of the ship is in the lead but it also must displace the resistance of a good deal of water and is the ship's first point of contact with rough seas. It is what enables the ship to cut through deep, even troubled waters well, but it also must bear the brunt of whatever unseen hazards the great sea has waiting for it. The authority the preacher carries into that pulpit is no lighthearted matter. The prudent preacher will carry a life jacket into that pulpit on Sunday morning as well and also make sure that there is enough ballast there to provide stability should the need arise.

In the context of the worshipping community the preacher is not only the authority figure and bearer of the sacred, she is also the carrier of dignity for the gathered people. This is why even modestly inappropriate behavior on the preacher's part can be unsettling and offensive. There is an appropriateness to the leadership of worship that excludes improper language, posture, or gesture. The preacher just isn't going to sit in the chancel area and have a cigarette before preaching or tell a questionable double-entendre story from the pulpit or pick her nose during the sermon hymn—or should I say I hope that the preacher wouldn't do such things. There simply are certain behaviors that are inappropriate for someone entrusted with carrying the dignity of the gathered people into the presence of God. The people have vested a good deal of trust and authority in the preacher for this very task, and it is not only grossly inappropriate but also fool-hardy to violate that trust.

In assuming the leadership role in the worship service the preacher also has assumed a significant level of responsibility for others. It is this responsibility for rather than authority over others that preachers are most likely to resist. To have people follow your lead is one thing; to be responsible for and accountable to God for these same people when they do so is quite another matter. The authority vested in the preaching office is primarily of this second type: responsibility for rather than power over people. The distinction is an important one for preachers to remember.

The decisive question for preachers then becomes how to assume such responsibility for others without also assuming authoritarian power over them at the same time. Well, one thing that assuming such responsibility means for preachers is a willingness to stand behind their own words and deeds. But this willingness is something quite different from the sort of pseudo claiming of responsibility that some American politicians have engaged themselves in during these last years. Often one after another of them will, with great fanfare and forthrightness, admit responsibility for some untoward action or decision, but then that's the end of it. There is no piper to be paid. In fact such *mea culpa* behavior appears often to be calculated to work in the politician's favor in the polls or on Election Day.

For stewards of the gospel, however, this ought not be so. To assume responsibility before God for others means, first and foremost, a willingness to stand under God's discerning judgment concerning one's stewardship of that responsibility, which has nothing to do with voter surveys, opinion polls, or focus groups and everything to do with accountability, confession, forgiveness, and grace. To assume responsibility before God for others further means that the spiritual health and well-being of those others is a matter of central importance to the preacher, much more so than is the preacher's ranking in the congregation's opinion polls or even her chance of reelection. Pastoral authority as a sense of responsibility for the spiritual health and guidance of others is not a matter for calculation and manipulation. It is a fundamental matter of pastoral integrity, authenticity, and authority being enacted at their deepest and fullest levels of meaning and possibility.

The mystery of the authority of the preaching office is simply expressed in the Helvetica Posterior: *"Praedicatio verbi dei est verbum dei,"* that is, the congregation believes it encounters the presence of God in the words of the preacher. That is perhaps in some ways a daunting message to earnest preachers who believe it but who also sense so little positive effect roused by their own preaching. Yet, all of us, and the whole church, can take heart and find encouragement in Jesus' own two "three-word" sermons to his disciples following his resurrection: First: "Be not afraid," and second, "I send you." In that command and in that promise are our own encouragement, our hope, and our authority to preach in Jesus' name.

# 3

# VALUING THE LISTENER
## CURIOSITY AND INDEFINITENESS
## IN ADDRESSING THE HEAD
## AND THE HEART

*ঔ৫*

The authority of the minister of the Word is manifest in
his leaving only partly described what can only be partly described, no matter how disappointed or distressed
his hearers may be. Every authentic proclamation of the
Gospel has always a definite indefiniteness about it.

R. E. C. BROWNE
*The Ministry of the Word*

## Valuing the Listener

Listeners are essential partners in preaching. Without
them what the preacher says isn't a sermon but a
soliloquy, like discoursing to oneself on the stage of an
empty theater. Yet preaching at times can be much like
a soliloquy—a solo performance—even when the sanctuary is full, and that simply is poor preaching regard-

59

less of the elocutionary skill or even the sincerity of the preacher. What moves the sermon from observed performance to shared enterprise is the valuing of the listeners by the preacher and the preacher's curiosity about their response to what is being said. In the preaching act itself, the preacher's valuing of the listener as a partner is an important factor in sustaining the vitality and movement of the sermon from beginning to end.

In his book *Who Needs God*, Rabbi Harold Kushner describes how Martin Buber makes a distinction between talking "*about* other people, relating to them as objects, thinking only of how they can be useful to us," and talking "*to* them, being aware of their presence, their feelings, seeing them as subjects in their own right."[1] Kushner gives as a clear example of this distinction the familiar Twenty-third Psalm, where the psalmist speaks about God both as an object ("He") and as a real presence ("Thou"). At the psalm's opening are the several well-known "He" references: "He makes me lie down in green pastures. . . . He leads me beside still waters. . . . He restores my soul. . . . He leads me in right paths . . ." Then, following the psalmist's statement of human vulnerability, "Even though I walk through the darkest valley," comes the statement concerning God's real presence in the psalmist's life, "I fear no evil; for you ("Thou" in the KJV) are with me" (Psalm 23:1-4).

Kushner points out further that "Buber defines *religion* as experiencing God and *theology* as talking about God." For Buber, this difference is like the difference between having dinner and reading a menu;[2] or, as Soren Kierkegaard elsewhere puts it, commenting on the Danish preachers of his time, their preaching was like reading the cookbook to someone who was starving. Being truly curious about the sermon's listeners is the homiletical difference between having dinner and reading the menu, between reading the cookbook and starving, between Buber's definition of religion and his definition of theology. When the listener feels recognized and valued as an essential factor in the preaching act, he will become much more present to and engaged in the sermon, just as is true of people participating in normal conversation. It is when people sense themselves to be valued participants in the conversation and not simply passive receptacles for someone else's opinions and biases that they willingly, often energetically, become engaged in it themselves, because now they are active in the conversation and no longer just observing it. The preacher's valuing of the listener in this way first of all honors the presence of Christ in that person and so further validates the centrality of the incarnational nature of Christianity. It also leads the listeners to pay more careful attention to what is being said because the listeners sense both that the speaker is interested in them and that something is being asked of them. They are part of this thing too.

One of the most effective ways to engage the listener as an active participant in the sermon is to speak to the listener's heart *and* to allow the heart room to respond. The same is true of the listener's mind. Allowing the heart and the mind room to respond is as important as speaking to them both in the first place. This opportunity for internal response is an important part of the sermon's work, and the responding is done by the listener. By allowing room for the listener's response I don't mean room simply to agree or disagree with the preacher's thought, although that is part of it. I mean also room for the inner response evoked in the listener by what the preacher has said. And by allowing room I don't mean literally pausing for a few seconds while speaking. Rather I mean something much more subtle and real—listening for the listener's response, being curious about it and valuing it, even as you are speaking. It is not a matter of homiletical technique. It is a matter of character and of pastoral care in the pulpit. In the privacy of the counseling chamber while speaking to a troubled parishioner the compassionate pastor likely will be keenly interested in how that person is responding on the inside to what the pastor is saying. The pastor communicates this through authentic presence, focused attention, and real interest in the parishioner's response even while the pastor is speaking. These same principles can be applied to the sanctuary on Sunday morning. Authentic presence, focused attention, and real interest in the people's presence in the sanctuary with the preacher are basic building blocks for any structure of substance the preacher may hope to build through the sermon. If the people know from the outset that they are valued and that something will be expected of them in this sermon too and that, in the best sense, someone is "watching them" as they listen, there is a much better chance that they will not only listen to but also participate in the sermon and, when it is finished, feel valued in having done so.

A second effective way to engage the listener as a participant in the sermon is not to speak to the mind exclusively, thus signaling from the outset that a cerebral response is not the only response being sought by the preacher. George MacDonald, a nineteenth-century Christian writer and poet, addresses this concern in a passage titled "Influences," in which he says, "It is not necessary that the intellect should define and separate before the heart and soul derive nourishment. As well say that a bee can get nothing out of a flower," he goes on, "because she does not understand botany. The very music of the stately words of such a poem [Milton's *Comus*] is enough to generate a better mood, to make one feel the air of higher regions, and wish to rise 'above the smoke and stir of this dim spot.' " He goes on to say that "the best influences which bear upon us" are often "of this vague sort." They are powerful influences "on the heart and conscience, although undefined to the intellect."[3] Anyone who has ever loved somebody knows what that means.

This is not an appeal to anti-intellectualism but an appeal to a balance of intellect and feeling. It is also to say that the heart knows things the mind does not know and that both the heart and the mind need to be engaged in the most effective holistic communication from the pulpit.

A third effective way to engage the listener as a participant in the sermon is to speak to the common memory of our human experience. Take, for instance, a sermon that has in it the idea of giving children both "roots and wings." In describing mother and father at home some months after the wedding of a much loved daughter, happy for her but missing her dearly, the preacher, as Fred Craddock has done, describes the father getting dressed one evening to go out to dinner. As he dresses, some dried grains of rice fall out of the cuff of his suit pants—the same suit he wore at the wedding. He sits on the edge of the bed and tears well up in his eyes. When his wife sits down next to him and asks what's wrong, he doesn't say a word. He simply uncurls his fist and shows her the grains of rice. Then they embrace and both weep quietly.

Now, not everyone in the sanctuary that day has to have had that very experience in order to be able to get something out of it, to have some memory of loss or change, of that perplexing human experience of sadness and joy coexisting, evoked in them. If the story conveys real human experience and emotion, then the memory seeks out its own comparable experience and suitable response. The listeners don't even have to be married, let alone have a child in order to have their own experience of the memory of a painful loss or a difficult change or life adjustment evoked in them. And the preacher doesn't have to add any word of instruction in the sermon either, as in "Dear friends, you may not be married or have children, but yet we all . . . etc." Trust the listeners to do that work themselves. They need no further guidance from the preacher, and if they do, then the story didn't have enough size to it, enough room in it, enough truth to it, for them to find their own place.

A fourth effective way to engage the listener as a participant in the sermon is to remember and acknowledge the fact that even statements as apparently obvious in meaning as "Christ is Risen" or "Jesus is Lord" are also profound mysteries, and the preacher should not pretend or assume otherwise. Name the preacher who understands just what it is he is saying when he proclaims the great Easter gospel, "He is not here. He is risen" or when he speaks the words "The body of Christ given for you. The blood of Christ shed for you" at the communion rail. For the preacher to acknowledge such profound mysteries is also to allow the listeners to acknowledge them. And it further allows them both to realize that in the vastness of our human experience there is always someone who has experience of the opposite of what we assume to be the "eternal truths." Take "God is love" for instance. Well, that is true enough by any reasonable standard, it seems. The problem for some people, however, is that their lives haven't fallen into the pleasant lines of reasonable standards. A child is raped. A young mother dies a painful death. A husband is both unfaithful and abusive. A teenage daughter who has never had sex contracts HIV from a blood transfusion during an operation. Sometimes the experience of people like this leads them to the understandable belief that there is truth, at least the truth of their own experience, also expressed in the opposite of some of the eternal truths. This isn't to say that "God is indifference." But it is to say that such a feeling is, in fact, the sense of God that sorely pressed, decent people, people who even want to believe differently, sometimes honestly have. And it is a great disservice to them to speak as though these great truths are so self-evidently true as to allow for no other consideration. What, I have from time to time wondered, does a preacher who can cavalierly mouth the "eternal truths" do with Jesus' own great, wrenching puzzlement over one such truth—the assumed benevolent presence of God—when he cries out from the cross, "My God, My God, why have you forsaken me?" (Matthew 27:46). No, in the real world and for the wise and compassionate preacher, valuing the listener also means understanding and acknowledging that "Christ is risen" is heard quite differently by someone sitting in church on Easter morning who has just been diagnosed with a terminal illness or someone who, after worship, will travel to the cemetery to place fresh flowers on a newly dug grave than it is by someone whose life is set in pleasant pathways at the moment. It means that "Jesus wept" is heard quite differently by someone who can't stop crying than it is by someone who can't understand why other people do. It means that "Jesus is Lord" is more than a bumper-sticker slogan to someone whose life is falling apart and who is struggling even to want to stay alive and for whom the saying of those words is both encouragement and puzzlement, to whom they seem both true and false at the same time. Or consider what Paul's insight that "love never ends" sounds like to someone recently divorced who didn't want to be. The valuing of dear vulnerable people such as these in preaching means, in part, loving them and accepting them and saying for them some things that their own hearts are, that day, too wounded to say.

## Being Curious

When someone leaving church on Sunday morning says to the preacher at the door, "You spoke to me today," they mean, at least in part, that the preacher valued them in some way by taking their presence that day into consideration. Those addressed by the sermon are, in this sense, its second center, that is, they are those who long to be personally spoken to, not literally but *feelingfully,* in the sermon. The communication dynamic at work in such a setting is that of the preacher truly seeking the other person not as an admirer or a receiver of the preacher's ideas, but as an active, valued, and engaged participant in the sermon's silent dialogue between the preacher and the listeners.

Just as the personal pronoun *I* belongs to the preacher's genuineness, so too does the pronoun *you* belong in reference to the preacher's listeners. The frequency of the use of *you* in addressing the listener is generally a good indication of whether and to what extent the preacher intends to include the listener in the sermon's silent dialogue and to take the listener seriously as a nonverbal but engaged participant in the sermon. Yet often an entire worship service can occur with the only use of *you* taking place in the liturgy, such as in "I baptize you . . ." or "The body of Christ given for you . . ." or "The Lord bless you and keep you . . ." or perhaps in some hymn verses.

The ever popular and ubiquitous homiletical *we* often replaces not only the *I* of the preacher but also the *you* of the listener as well. Following this approach, no actual human being present either has to speak directly (thus risking disclosure) or be addressed directly (thus risking confrontation). The ubiquitous and frequently unctuous *we* thus easily can become demonic by subtly robbing the sermon of its power to confront the conscience, convict the heart, and compel the volition in the silent but dynamic exchange between the one who speaks directly and the many who listen as though they are, in fact, being personally addressed.

Another way to be curious about the listeners and to take their presence seriously is not to assume what their responses are going to be or, worse, to speak their response for them. Homiletical examples of this presumption abound: "As all of us would agree," "As everyone knows," "We've all felt from time to time," "None of you would agree with me, but . . ." Actual listener's responses to statements such as those vary widely but even if one of them might happen to be true, it is, nevertheless, not the preacher's place to form it. That is the work of the listener and the Holy Spirit. Both yes and no have to be viable options for the listeners. The preacher must value and practice this too, if genuine response to the sermon is to be possible, because among the most common practical effects of the homiletical *we* is the forced inclusion of the listeners into the preacher's opinions and biases. This is at least presumptuous, often arrogant, and regularly simply inaccurate. "We've all lost that childlike Christmas joy" or "We all like to blame others for our problems" or "We all know what it's like to be young and foolish" are examples of such statements, which simply are not universally true of all human beings, including those present in the sanctuary at the time. Some present have never lost childlike Christmas joy and some perhaps never had it to start with. Some never blame anyone but themselves. Some aren't even old enough yet to have had a chance to be young and foolish and some are now perhaps too old to remember that they ever were so. Such uses of the homiletical *we* often actually are unintended revealing statements of disclosure concerning the preacher much more than they are accurate statements about the listeners. In many cases the *we* really should be *I* with the *I* being the preacher, who lost his childlike wonder at the marvel of Christmas or her sense of youthful exuberance and is either resentful or trying to find it again.

If the listeners don't really see themselves in statements like these then they experience themselves to be illegitimately included in something they never subscribed to in the first place and will, rightly, begin to resist the preacher at other points as well, points at which they really ought to be involved. The really serious problem in the preacher's failure to be curious about the listener's actual experiences and responses is that it can lead the preacher routinely to make unwarranted assumptions about the listener's experiences, thoughts, and preferences that, in turn, can create great distance between the listeners and the preacher and, sadly, also between the listeners and any legitimate gospel word the preacher may speak. So, instead of saying, on the Second Sunday of Easter, when the gospel lesson is about "Doubting Thomas," "We all have trouble having to live by faith instead of sight," it would likely be both more accurate and honest for the preacher to say, "I know I'm with Thomas a lot of the time. I have some trouble living by faith rather than sight myself. Do you?" This approach lacks the arrogance of the homiletical *we;* it speaks a clear word of appropriate, honest self-disclosure; and it is curious about the listener's experience rather than assuming to know what it is. This approach also values and includes the listeners in the sermon's dynamic silent dialogue rather than presuming to pigeonhole them into a category of response in which perhaps no one, except the preacher, is actually located. Some precious old valiant soul there may have walked by faith with great courage all her days. She needs to know that because the pastor and Thomas share the same dilemma doesn't mean there is something wrong with her if she doesn't. She may just be ahead of them both in that regard.

With all of this said, however, it is still the preacher's inner attitude, not the preacher's use of proper pronouns, that is the decisive factor. It is not, finally, a matter of grammar, syntax, or technique. It is rather a matter of the heart's desire to be inclusive and to communicate to others honestly, compassionately, authentically, and effectively. It is a matter of so valuing those who are listening to the sermon as to include them as actual, if silent, partners in its creation rather than simply passive absorbers of its presentation. Being truly curious about their inner responses to what is being said is a good place to start in concretely valuing them, their presence, their participation, and their response. Without such active engagement between the preacher and the listeners, the sermon truly does become a soliloquy—the sad image of the preacher talking to himself on an empty stage with no one else there. And I use the word *sad* advisedly, because when the gospel is the message not being heard it is a very sad matter altogether.

My own experience as a preacher regularly teaches me that people are looking much more for salvation than they are for information when they enter the sanctuary for Sunday worship. By this I mean that they are looking for wholeness, for a word that connects them more deeply to that which eludes and transcends them. Although they might not say it, or even consciously realize it, they are seeking an experience of the holy—a capacity to see the extraordinary presence of God in the ordinary events of their lives. I believe they are much more concerned with such vague but powerful urges than they are with the preacher's finely honed insights or ability to persuade. It is the preacher who feels compelled to come up with a startlingly new insight about the meaning of Christmas each year, not the parishioners. I believe the great majority of them would be content with a simple well-told retelling of the "old, old story" with appropriate references to the connection between its marvelous mystery and the marvelous mystery of their own lives. After all, the Christmas story isn't the preacher's story; it's the church's story. The preacher doesn't need to make up a new version of it every year. The people already know it. Yet more interesting facts about just when or where the birth actually occurred aren't at the heart of the matter. God's great self-emptying *(kenosis)* in the incarnation of Jesus is the heart of the matter. Preachers who tell that story faithfully and well say all that needs to be said because the story itself places them and the people closer to wonder, holiness, and mystery. The people are, themselves, capable of drawing meaning from the story and applying it to their lives. Trust them to do so.

The mystery of the encounter in proclamation takes on concrete form in the dynamic relationship *between* the preacher and the listener, not *from* the active preacher to the passive listener. For most listeners the effect of the sermon is inseparably connected with the effect of the preacher. Theologians and homileticians frequently focus on the intellectual content of the sermon, that is, on its "meaning" and theological correctness. This, of course, has its appropriate and necessary place. However, in order for that "correct" content to have significance for the listener, that significance must occur first within the framework of the relationship between the listener and the preacher. This relationship between preacher and listener is a key ingredient influencing the effectiveness of the worship service upon its participants. Any cognitive truth witnessed to in worship also must be communicated affectively in order to be most fully received. It is here where a relationship of openness and trust between the one who speaks and the many who hear becomes essential to effective communication. Within the context of preaching, "truth" is more personally communicative than it is simply cognitive. If the preacher does not, first of all, speak in a way that is trustworthy, authentic, and believable, then no matter how clever or thoughtful or even sincere his ideas might be, they will not be fully heard or received or responded to by the listener if the listener does not also sense himself or herself to be personally addressed. This does not mean actually addressed as "Bob" or "Sheila" in the sermon but addressed in the sense of being valued and taken seriously as a partner with the preacher in the sermon's work.

All of this is certainly not to say that the preacher is more important than the text in preaching. This is clearly not so. It does say, however, that the preacher possesses something the text does not: corporality, and that is a significant difference. The preacher has a human body, a voice, a personality, a history, a heart, and a mind through which the text is presented to the people. The listener's primary experience of the sermon's biblical text is not as words on a page or as a theological abstraction but as a living encounter communicated through the physical presence—the body, the heart, the mind—of the preacher. For the preacher to be curious about the listener's response to his presence, then, is not only a vain or practical concern. It is a theological and spiritual concern as well, because the listener's response to the preacher's presence is so closely related to the listener's receptivity toward or resistance to hearing the text and participating in the sermon. Preaching truly is an incarnate presentation of the word and in that sense, as noted earlier, a sacramental one as well. Such an understanding can be an encouragement for preachers no less than for those to whom they preach. To be the presence of Christ for one another surely ought to encourage both preachers and listeners to be attentive toward and curious about one another in loving, compassionate, and thoughtful ways. It is, after all, Christ himself in us who is being so honored when this is done. Kathleen Norris, pondering a response to Rainer Maria Rilke's poetic question, "Who is this Christ, who interferes in everything?" tells of a time once when she was the only guest at a women's monastery. The sisters invited her to join them in the community's Sunday evening procession into church. That procession became for her "a reminder of the procession of life itself" because the older and more infirm sisters with their walkers and canes went first, setting a pace the other women had to follow. The prioress and Norris brought up the rear. As they began to move, the prioress whispered to Norris, "We bow first to the Christ who is at the altar . . . and then we turn to face our partner, and bow to the Christ in each other."[4] This is an apt description of the healthy spiritual dynamic to be sought, nurtured, and honored between preacher and listeners gathered together for worship—

both acknowledging the transcendent presence of Christ beyond their knowing and the imminent presence of Christ right there among them when they look into one another's eyes and listen to one another's voices. Being curious about things such as these is active spiritual discipline of a high order and potentially also of great blessing for both preacher and listener alike.

Being curious also means that the preacher develops a sense for the questions of the listener. "How are they hearing this?" "What does it mean to them?" "Where will they resist this message?" "Where will they welcome it?" These are the types of questions the preacher should have in mind even while speaking. There is, then, a sense in which an important function of the preacher is to represent the listeners as they listen to the sermon. This doesn't mean that the preacher literally begins each sermon with rhetorical or leading questions put to the listeners or that sermons assume a question-and-answer format. Rather, the preacher's questioning is an internal matter in which he wonders actively but silently about the listener's responses to what is being said when the sermon is being delivered. The purpose of such a discipline on the preacher's part is not to help the preacher make midstream corrections whenever he looks out and sees befuddled looks on the faces in the pews (although that couldn't hurt from time to time) but rather to help the preacher value the listeners more intentionally and concretely as participants in the sermon. Preachers who aren't curious about their listeners in a manner such as this can at times invent an audience for their sermons that isn't actually there.

Being genuine, speaking in a clear, direct, unaffected manner, assuming responsibility before God for one's own self and for one's listeners, and being curious about those listeners are all factors in the preacher's effective communication of the gospel. Of course content is never to be slighted, but that content's effectiveness includes these other matters as well. Again, as the novelist Saul Bellow so clearly stated, "abstractions will not travel" by themselves; "they must pass through the heart to be transmitted." If this is true of our normal daily relationships, surely it is also true of our relationship with God in Christ and of our relationships with one another as members of the mystical Body of Christ, the Church.

All of this is to say that the proclamation of the gospel through preaching has an unavoidable, glorious human component: human flesh, human thought, human history, human emotion, human frailty and vulnerability, human words. In this century, under the influence of the students of Karl Barth and Emil Brunner, theological understanding of the word became so central that the experience of the word began to atrophy or to be taken over primarily by charismatic or Pentecostal preachers who often erred in the opposite direction by emphasizing emotion at the expense of sound theological understanding. From a homiletical perspective each of these understandings is capable of moving toward a healthier, more vital spiritual center in which carefully discerned theological insight is not lost in abstraction but rather effectively communicated from both the mind and the heart of the preacher to the mind and the heart of the listener.

## On Not Being Too Clear

Having spoken of the importance of clarity in preaching it is appropriate to say a brief word about untidiness as well. These two words do not clash nearly as much as at first they may appear to. In speaking of clarity I have meant to encourage the preacher not to equivocate. I have not intended to use the word in the sense of precision or exactitude with all of one's thoughts and themes in preaching. In using the word *untidy* now I mean to encourage the preacher not to get everything too clear, so neatly wrapped up and presented as to leave the listener no room for response. Surety may be what we long for, but uncertainty is what we mostly get in life as we actually live it. The concept of untidiness in the preaching office is intended to address that felt discrepancy between desire and reality honestly and pastorally.

R. E. C. Browne, in his chapter on the essential untidiness of preaching, says, "The tidy mind is not the truthful mind; the utterance that leaves no room for doubt or place for question is the fruit of a mind that is full of unwarranted conclusions."[5] The task of the faithful preacher, then, is deliberately to preserve an "untidy mind" so as to maintain an internal honesty about the ambiguities of daily life as it is actually experienced, both by him and by those to whom he preaches. There is an intellectual honesty and humility at work in such an approach too because an openness to untidiness begins with the acknowledgment that the conclusions of all human thought are tentative. Only God can see the whole fabric of creation. Any finite being, including every preacher, will of necessity leave things out of even his deepest consideration because the existence of them is unknowable or hidden from him.

It is because we don't like uncertainty and fear the unknown that we are constantly tempted to make our minds and thus our worlds "tidy," that is, predictable and knowable, thereby attempting to sustain the illusion that the world and our experience in it are also then controllable. It is our human abhorrence of arbitrariness, of the apparent fickleness and whimsy of nature, that we wish to tidy up with certain assurances, divine or otherwise. The "otherwise" is where the preacher's temptation, often rooted in noble feelings of compassion and care for his listeners, becomes quite real. In order to comfort and reassure people it is a great temptation to speak with confidence and surety about things that no human being really knows for sure. And even the well-intended preacher becomes dishonest—perhaps unknowingly, but dishonest nonetheless—when he speaks tidily about things that are, and will remain, to our human purview essentially untidy.

The nature of language itself is a factor in the essential untidiness of preaching because there is no direct one-to-one corollary between the symbol of the word and its reference. When the preacher speaks of such things as love or will or character or joy, he cannot speak unequivocally because there are no entities exactly corresponding to love or will or character or joy in the real world. Rather, there are literally millions of "for instances" of each of them and each of those is constantly changing and adapting. As R. E. C. Browne succinctly puts it, "Untidiness of mind could only be banished at the expense of truth; silence would be the only way to avoid ambiguity in speech."[6] In other words, even the preacher's most accurate and honest statements are always actually only the nearest and best approximations the preacher can make. They can never fully incapsulate the truth. They can only point in its direction, and even then often, as Emily Dickinson put it, only in a slanted way.

In this regard two unlikely bedfellows, scientists and poets, can be the preacher's tutors. The best scientists will look at the world in wonder and say they aren't claiming to give a literal description of the universe and that their most accurate and sensitive measurements are no more than the nearest approximations at which they can arrive. And the greatest poets will say they never mean exactly what they say simply because they can never say exactly what they mean. Isn't that the preacher's dilemma too? How can we preachers say exactly who God is? We can say "look to Jesus" but then we've only really pointed in the direction of the great eternal incarnational mystery of God in human flesh. We can fall back to the doctrine of the trinity, but what human mind has ever fully comprehended that profound mystery that the Godhead consists of a community of persons, three in one? This is not yet to mention love or suffering or death or eternity or why the sun rises or the wind blows or the human heart beats, for that matter. It is, all of it, in the end a grand, profound glorious mystery in the face of which silence and reverence are the first and most appropriate responses. It is out of such silence and reverence that the preacher begins to realize the profundity of the preaching task and that everything he says is, at best, an approximate and necessarily untidy description of reality—whether the reality being described is the birth of creation or the birth of a baby. And then, out of that humbling knowledge, the preacher can dare to speak—not the whole truth of the sacred mysteries of faith and of life, but the truth as he in his own untidiness has come to know it.

There is wisdom for the preacher in Baron von Hügel's counsel to his niece:

> Never get things too clear. Religion can't be clear. In this mixed-up life there is always an element of unclearness. . . . If I could understand religion as I understand that two and two makes four, it would not be worth understanding. Religion can't be clear if it is worth having. To me, if I can see things through, I get uneasy—I feel it's a fake. I know I have left something out, I've made some mistake.[7]

# 4

# HOW TO DEVELOP THE HEAD AND HEART CONNECTION

*৶৶*

Do not speak unless you can improve on the silence.
A BUDDHIST MONK

## Listening to the Text: Silence

Not speaking unless we can improve on the silence is counsel that would leave me and many of the preachers I know dumbstruck on most Sunday mornings and at various other times as well. Often we preachers do not believe that our own speech is improving on the silence out of which it comes, yet we have been called, trained, certified, and ordained to preach—to break the silence with some regularity, at least each Sunday morning. Therefore it is prudent for us not only to consider our words carefully but also to pay attention to the silence out of which they come and in which they are formed.

Wilhelm Löhe, a nineteenth-century German divine, commenting in *The Lutheran Pastor* on the necessity of private devotions and the development of an inner life of prayer for the pastor, observes that "whoever must always give must always have; and since he cannot draw out of himself what he must give, he must ever keep near the living fountain in order to draw. . . . The fulness and consecration of life is a praying heart. Solitude is the fountain of all living streams, and nothing glorious is born in public."[1] An attentive silence in solitude is the appropriate starting place in the process of preparation for preaching. Such silence in solitude precedes even active petitionary prayer seeking the guidance of the Holy Spirit in the sermon's preparation, because it is out of attentive silence in solitude that such prayer can most accurately and honestly be formed. Asking for help before attempting to discern what is needed is a short-circuiting of spiritual discipline and accountability before God. To say that nothing glorious is born in public is to acknowledge that discipline and hard work are required by the preacher's craft and also to acknowledge the preacher's dependency on the guidance and grace of God for the development and delivery of any God-pleasing sermon.

The fundamental medium for all sound is silence. Silence is not what occurs when there is no sound. Rather, silence is the one constant medium into which a multiplicity of sounds, including the human voice, continuously breaks. When the preacher speaks from the pulpit she too is breaking the silence with the spoken word. Speech then becomes the fundamental human sacrament by which the silence is broken and the people addressed by the preacher with the word.

Garrison Keillor, American humorist, master storyteller, and the host of the National Public Radio program *A Prairie Home Companion,* says of his own creative process and the response of people to it that "silence is a profound stimulant to people of imagination."[2] He says this, in part, in relationship to his own creative process of storytelling and, in part, in relationship to the intentional uses of silence within the stories as he is telling them, thereby also allowing for silences out of which his listeners have evoked in them memories or emotions that have not been placed there by Keillor but rather emerge from the silence and the context in which it is shared between him and them. This seems to me to be helpful information for the preacher too, as well as potentially beneficial to the preacher's listeners. Silence can serve as the medium in which the heart's memory and the soul's longing can have their presence acknowledged and valued and given time and space in which to emerge. This may not always be some lovely thought or feeling. Yet it likely will be some inner dynamic, be it fear or pain or puzzlement or sorrow, that nevertheless needs to be heard and attended to before wholeness and inner peace can become truly possible. Silence may not always evoke the pleasant, but it can evoke, with clarifying regularity, the necessary. That reality, although at times painful, much like the lancing of a festering boil, can become the beginning of relief and healing and of the restoration of hope and possibility.

Blaise Pennington somewhere tells of a time once when someone who had heard him preach in person and was greatly moved by his sermon invited him to preach on a BBC religious program. He accepted the invitation to do so and preached over the air the same sermon that had so impressed his host in person. Following the broadcast the host seemed somewhat disappointed and said that the sermon just didn't seem the same to him somehow. This puzzled Pennington some-what, as he thought he'd preached exactly the same sermon the man had heard in church. It was only later, when Pennington himself listened to a recording of the radio broadcast, that he realized what had happened. Due to the time constraints of fitting a Bible lesson, an anthem, and announcements into a thirty-minute pro-gram, the radio editors had removed all of the silences from the sermon. Those silences were, to Pennington, essential to the overall message he was presenting and their removal gave the sermon not only a decidedly dif-ferent pace but also a clearly different effect. His disap-pointed host was, in fact, right. He had heard two distinctly different sermons. And although he likely didn't realize it, the single most significant difference was the absence of silence. In the first sermon he was a valued listener whose response was sought and given space to respond. In the second sermon he was viewed much more as a passive observer and receiver of information. Little wonder that those two sermons seemed so differ-ent to him because, of course, they were. Silence can be a profound stimulant to the human heart and mind and soul. It allows people to respond to preaching in an interior way that fills the silence not with the preacher's continuous exhortation to do or to be one thing or another but rather allows the silence to swell with the inner response of the listener's own heart and mind and volition.

For the early monastic communities silence was a presence, not simply an absence of noise and sound. The fourth-century desert Copts were mostly ignorant of Greek philosophy but knew much of the Bible, espe-cially the psalms, by heart. When Evagrius, a man who was well-educated and literate in Greek, came to the desert to live as a monk, he asked one of the elder monks to advise him: "Tell me some piece of advice by which I might be able to save my soul," he said. The elder monk replied: "If you wish to save your soul, do not speak unless you are asked a question." Being an educated and articulate man, this advice proved difficult for Evagrius to follow, and he soon violated it by offering his own counsel at one of the meetings of the monks. Again one of the elders took him aside and told him he needed to learn how to listen and be silent. This time he took the advise: "You are right, my fathers. I have spoken once; I will not do so a second time." By the time of his death, Evagrius had himself become a revered elder in the community in large measure due to the fact they he had learned the importance of speaking only out of his own deep and honored silence.[3] Such a lesson is a timely one for stewards of the gospel in every generation.

All of our human speech is born in silence, and our thoughtful, gracious words are formed in it. Speech is actually a very physical activity. It requires both a human voice—shaped by lips, tongue, and larynx—to be spoken and a human ear—shaped by the hammer, anvil, and stirrup—to be heard. Our words, then, are indeed deeds. To form and to speak them thoughtfully and effectively is a matter of central importance for the preacher. Words are not harmless. They can carry great blessing or cause great and lasting harm, and often do. So, to be intentional, reflective, and judicious about their use in preaching is an essential pastoral, spiritual, and theological matter. To reflect upon their use in silence, before they are ever uttered from the pulpit, is a responsible act of pastoral care, spiritual discipline, and theological discernment. It is clear that Jesus himself knew the importance of "mere words" when, in Matthew, he warned, "On the day of judgment you will have to give an account for every careless word you utter; for by your words you will be justified, and by your words you will be condemned" (Matthew 12:36-37). The prudent, thoughtful, and reflective use of words is the wisest course to follow, especially for those entrusted with the stewardship of the gospel, whose final reckoning before God will include an accounting of every thoughtful and every careless word they have ever spoken or left unspoken. Given this inevitability, there is both wisdom and prudence in the preacher's listening carefully in silence before she utters a single word. According to Jesus, God is listening to and remembering them all even when the preacher is not.

I am myself regularly convicted by the sage counsel of the Buddhist monk, "Do not speak unless you can improve on the silence." Each time I finish preaching or teaching or counseling and then reflect on what I've said and failed to say, I realize just how poorly I have followed its wisdom. I believe that most preachers join me in not enjoying having their intellectual inadequacies and spiritual immaturities paraded before others regularly. Often I feel as though I can offer no improvement on the silence, and yet I speak. I preach because I have been called by the people I serve in Christ to do so. My inner sense that silence would be better than my speech is especially keen at occasions such as funerals, but it is also true of each approaching Sabbath. I don't believe I am alone among preachers when I often embarrass myself with the inadequacies of my own thought and speech when I know the need for guidance, encouragement, and healing is so deep and so real in the lives of those to whom I speak and for whom I care so dearly.

Yet, most thoughtful pastors also can recall times when they should have spoken up but didn't. Silence such as that is neither a virtue nor a blessing. It is a lack of integrity and courage. I know this from my own failure to speak this way. We are probably much less likely to recall times when we should have been silent but did not restrain ourselves from speaking. There are times when the hardest thing to do is to listen attentively to another, which requires of us at least this one thing clearly: that we are not speaking. Silence is the medium that allows true spiritual space to be filled by the presence of another. This is, perhaps, why Zechariah was made mute by Gabriel in Luke 1:20, and why we preachers too might more wisely cultivate the interior gift of times of appropriate muteness as an important spiritual discipline in our own preaching preparation and pastoral care. By this I do not mean that we never speak or that we speak only tentatively and cautiously but rather that our speech, both in the pulpit and out of it, be brought into healthier balance and harmony with our silence.

The basic medium of all spoken communication is silence, into which we hurl all the words of poets and scientists and generals and preachers and lovers. Whenever we speak a word we break the fundamental silence. Isn't it wise then to have some principled sense of the appropriateness and propriety of the speech we use to break the silence that always envelops us?

The rabbis tell of one further detail of the ancient temple ceremony Zechariah was taking part in when he was struck mute that isn't in the Bible. It can remind us preachers yet today of the awesome, sacred nature of our pastoral commission to be faithful pastors and preachers of the gospel all our days. The story is this: Before the chosen priest went into the presence of the Lord, the other priests were to tie a rope around his leg so that if he were struck dead inside the sanctuary they could haul him out without risking destruction themselves.

Yes, indeed, fellow preachers: Do not speak unless you can improve on the silence.

## Engaging the Text: Method

Leading American choral director Robert Shaw, in describing the qualities essential to fine choral production, has said that "knowledge of fundamentals is prerequisite to free flight."[4] And Elton Trueblood in *The New Man for Our Time* has written, "We have not advanced very far in our spiritual lives if we have not encountered the basic paradox of freedom, to the effect that we are most free when we are bound. . . . With one concerted voice the giants of the devotional life apply the same principle to the whole of life with the dictum: *Discipline is the price of freedom.*"[5]

What is true for the musician and the theologian is also true for the preacher. Knowledge of the fundamentals of their craft is essential for preachers too, and discipline is as much the price of the preacher's freedom as it is for anyone whose task requires thought, preparation, and skill for its proper execution. To think otherwise is either to undervalue the task or to overvalue one's own capacity to accomplish it. Even the most gifted preachers weren't born that way. Rather, they have added to their natural gifts and desire a disciplined approach to their craft resulting in consistently meaningful and effective preaching. Most noted preachers will say that there is no "secret" to their success in preaching. For instance, I once heard Fred Craddock say of good preaching that its mother is hard work and its father is discipline. And I also once heard Gardner Taylor's response, given in a plenary session following a worship service in which he had preached, to a young preacher who commented on how "marvelously spontaneous" and "effortless" Taylor's sermon appeared to him to be. Taylor responded, with a flash in his eye and an ever so slight irritation in his voice, "Thank you. You pay me a high compliment—for you know there is an art that conceals art." He then went on to describe how for the first thirty-five years of his ministry there wouldn't have been four or five times that he did not painstakingly go through a demanding exegetical process from textual study to the development of a full written manuscript. His "marvelously spontaneous" sermon witnessed that day was the result of a long obedience in the same direction over decades of faithful pastoral care, hard work, and personal discipline. If such labor is required of the most highly skilled and gifted laborers in the vineyard, ought it not surely be at least as required of others of us who have also been called to the preaching office? There is at least this one sense in which "good luck" in preaching is related to "good luck" in most other fields of human endeavor: Good luck often is simply the point at which preparation meets opportunity. Or, as one insightful wit has put it, good luck is the residue of preparation.

For the parish pastor the point at which preparation can meet opportunity is a fixed recurring point at least once every week: Sunday morning. With that point clearly known to the preacher it is less than responsible not to anticipate it and to prepare for it as faithfully and well as possible. Key to such faithful and competent preparation is having a clearly defined method for approaching the task. Such a defined method can save both time and energy, which, in turn, can then more profitably be focused on the task itself rather than on wondering how to go about it. Although the tools of the preacher and the tools of the musician differ, Robert

Shaw's dictum also holds true of preaching: knowledge of fundamentals is prerequisite to free flight.

If a preacher doesn't know her destination it is highly unlikely that she will get there and if, by chance, she happens to do so, she probably won't realize that she has arrived. What was once whispered in a Scottish church by one weary parishioner to another in response to a question about when the preacher was going to finish, "He finished a long time ago, he just won't quit!" unfortunately is likely true of many American preachers as well. Far too many sermons are finished long after they are effectively done. One of the more helpful functions of following a disciplined method of preparation is knowing what it is you intended to say so that first you will say it, second you will recognize when you've said it, and third you will know much better when to stop saying it and conclude.

The method of textual study and sermon preparation outlined here owes a debt of recognition to my own gifted and generous teachers Fred B. Craddock and J. Phillip Swander.[6] The intention is to help bring clarity to what it is the preacher has to say and how to organize her thought most creatively in order to say it in the most effective and helpful way. The method assumes the use of a single biblical text as the focal point even if other texts are used to broaden or enlighten that focal point in the sermon.

It may seem silly or unnecessary to say it, but the very first step in sermon preparation is to read the text. As many seasoned preachers already know by experience, it is quite possible to work up a whole sermon without ever actually having read the text. "Oh, I know the parable of the Prodigal son by heart; now let's see, what in the world can I say about it this time?" No, the biblical text has a life and a voice of its own and the preacher is responsible for listening to that voice and not simply imposing her voice over it. Fred Craddock tells of one such time when he himself prepared a sermon on the text in Luke 15 about the hundred sheep and the shepherd going to look for the one that was lost. Having not read the text first, his sermon assumed that the ninety-nine were "safely in the fold," as an old gospel hymn has it, while the shepherd's search went on. What Luke actually says, however, is that the ninety-nine were left "in the wilderness" while the shepherd searched for that single lost one. When Craddock discovered that difference the whole tenor of the sermon changed and the old one had to be thrown out. Having read the text carefully made the difference. The sermon now was centered on high-risk love. The old sermon was useless. And there are many such partially remembered hymns and poems and old Sunday School stories lingering about that tempt preachers to flatter their memories but can do serious injustice to the actual biblical text.

A second reason for reading the text each time it is preached on is that the preacher is a different person than she was the last time the text was preached on and so a different capacity for insight and learning is brought to the reading, formed by the crucible of the preacher's own dynamic life experience between the time of the two readings. For instance, most preachers have preached on the baptism of Jesus by John in the Jordan River several times, as have I, and likely have followed predictable homiletical lines with it either about Jesus' relationship to John or his identity with sinful humankind. However, the last time I preached on this account from Matthew 3:13-17, after several oral readings of it, the first three words there stood out more clearly for me than they ever had before. Those three words, "Then Jesus came," led me in the direction of the nature of Jesus' obedience to his Father's will. This then led to other places in Matthew where Jesus showed similar obedience, to the Temptation story in Matthew 4 and then to Matthew 16, where Matthew reports, "From that time Jesus began to show his disciples that he must go to Jerusalem and suffer many things" (Matthew 16:21 RSV). A careful reading of the text led to the possibility of a new insight for preaching. That insight yet needed to be tested by careful exegesis, but at least a new possibility for faithful preaching had emerged from a direct engagement with the text itself.

A third reason for reading the text, and for reading it aloud during the process of preparation, is that this is the way the members of the early church first heard it and it is also the way the listeners will hear it on Sunday morning. Few of them will have given it much attention beforehand, so it is incumbent upon the preacher to have done so on their behalf. Their experience of the text is going to be an oral/aural one during the worship service. Rather than bemoaning that fact, a much more pastoral response is for the preacher to prepare for it intentionally and conscientiously so that the hearing of the text might bear the healthiest possible fruit in the lives of the listeners.

A second step in the sermon preparation process is to determine the boundaries of the text. Logically this step precedes step one in the study sequence because the proper text needs to be determined before being read and reflected upon. However, they are placed in this order so as to emphasize the central importance of actually reading the text at the beginning of the study process.

Determining the limits of the text means simply to ask if this pericope, as it now stands, is a whole textual unit. Or do verses need to be added or subtracted in order for the passage to make sense to the listeners? The preacher ought to be free to set the boundaries of text in her local situation, rather than having to unquestionably accept the boundaries as determined by a lectionary consultation committee some distance removed from the preacher's actual setting.

Having determined the appropriate limits of the text it is also important to review that text for any significant textual variants. Such variants often fall under the category of "other ancient authorities say" found in the footnotes of resources such as the New Oxford Annotated Bible. A reasonably responsible job of checking for any such significant variants in the text can be accomplished readily enough by using a sound and generally accessible resource such as Bruce Metzger's *Textual Commentary on the Greek New Testament*.

Having read the text itself and checked for its variants, a third step now becomes the reading of the text creatively, with what Fred Craddock and others, following Paul Ricoeur, calls a certain naivete. Such a reading precedes the use of commentary, dictionary, or lexicon and engages the preacher's own faith and heart and mind and memory with the text. At this point the focus is not on what the biblical scholars have to say about the text but on the preacher's own personal engagement with it. This can become a sacred, searching moment of encounter for the preacher. No one in human history has ever before had the precise combination of faith and doubt, of joy and sorrow, of success and failure, that each individual preacher brings to her encounter with the text. And there is no commentary or sermon illustration book that can provide that experience. Only the preacher can do so. The text has a life of its own and so does the preacher. To allow the life of the text to engage the life of the preacher is the beginning of an honest encounter that can lead to an honest, personal, insightful, and faithful proclamation of the gospel.

As the text is so read, record the thoughts, questions, images, intuitions, feelings, and memories that come to mind. Don't judge or qualify or puzzle over them too much. Simply keep track of them. Later they can be evaluated, enhanced or deleted. Such a direct engagement with the text has the ring of authenticity about it and the mark of personal integrity on it. It also provides for closer identity with the listeners because it allows the preacher to approach and experience the text in much the same way the listeners will on Sunday morning. Remember that their normal experience of any given text will be hearing it read aloud once on Sunday morning followed by whatever is evoked in them of remembrance, emotion, intuition, or puzzlement as they listen. The preacher's experiencing the text, insofar as it is possible in the same way the listeners will experience it, provides an opportunity for richer dialogue between the preacher and the listeners as partners in preaching.

Having read the text initially, established its boundaries and checked for its variants, and then read it a second time with an open naivete toward it, a fourth step in the process of sermon preparation now becomes the use of secondary sources such as commentaries, lexicons, and dictionaries. Such fine resources have their proper place and they ought to inform the preacher's study and preparation. But they ought also not be the whole of it, which is why they are placed here as step four in the preparation process. The preacher's temptation is to read what the biblical scholars have written on a given text and then to say, "What do I know in comparison with all these brilliant people?" The faithful response is that although those biblical scholars provide a great and necessary ministry to the church, none of them has been called to preach to or provide pastoral care for to the people to whom the preacher will speak on Sunday morning. Biblical scholars, church historians, and systematic theologians can supplement the preacher's knowledge, clarify the preacher's questions, and stimulate the preacher's mind, but they cannot preach the preacher's sermon. Only the preacher can do that.

Preachers can and ought to make use of biblical scholarship to expand their own mental horizons and deepen their scriptural knowledge and insight. However, it isn't appropriate to carry the notes from the study desk directly into the pulpit. Much of what is gained by reading commentaries and scholarly works ought to inform preaching but is not itself material for preaching. A different light shines on the Bible in the sanctuary than in the study. This is an important distinction for preachers to keep in mind.

Having completed a careful study of appropriate resources, a fifth step is now to approach the text again with this additional information and insight in mind. By now some of the initial questions of the text will have been answered and others will remain. Some of the initial images and memories and feelings will still seem appropriate and others will not. Such a rereading of the text following critical study of it helps bring clarity and focus to what is emerging as being of central and timely importance for the preaching of this particular text now, in the preacher's particular, unique setting.

Culling the initial responses to the text in this manner brings clarity to the sixth step in the process, which is to state in a single positive sentence what the text is saying, that is, to summarize the sermon's intended message in a simple declarative sentence. The task of the sermon then becomes how to form it so as to have the listeners effectively hear, understand, experience and respond to that message themselves. As much as is possible state this theme in positive terms. Say, for instance, "Do this and you will live" rather than "Don't do this and you will die." Both statements may reflect the truth, but the first one is more hopeful and encouraging and thus also stands a better chance of being heard and responded to positively.

Here are two of my own examples of the use of such focused statements arrived at following the process of textual study outlined above:

> Receptivity to the vulnerable is a sign of humility and of the movement of God's grace. Mark 9:30-37. This passage includes both the second passion prediction and Jesus' setting a child among his disciples as an illustration of the need for receptivity among them.

> It is the nature of the gospel that the initiative for reconciliation lies with the offended; or, forgiveness is not instinctive behavior, but it is something we can learn to do. Matthew 18:15-22. This passage, about community discipline among the early post-resurrection followers of Jesus, illustrates that different themes can be developed from the same text without losing the integrity of the text.

This single guiding theme becomes the message the preacher will want to present most clearly in the sermon. Of course having a clearly worded theme on paper and then being able to communicate that theme effectively are two separate matters. But without such a theme, resulting from demanding thought and faithful study, the preacher may well err in one of two significant ways. First, she may be less than faithful or accurate concerning the original intention of the text. And second, she may say little, if anything, that is clearly focused, biblically sound, and concretely related to the lives the sermon's listeners are actually living.

There is much more to sermon preparation than the study process outlined above. The theme carved out of textual study and personal reflection must now be crafted into a sermon for delivery. The development of the theme is the beginning point in the process of crafting a sermon, not the end point. How to craft a sermon so that the listeners are engaged in and respond to it with both their hearts and their minds is the topic to which we now turn our attention.

## Releasing the Text: Movement

Once the preacher has determined what is to be said, the task now becomes how best to say it. A key to this process is understanding the central importance of a sense of movement in the sermon, for it is this sense of movement that engages the listeners and keeps them working actively with the preacher throughout the sermon. As one seasoned preacher has put it: "If the people think you're going somewhere, they'll get on the bus." Developing such a sense of movement carrying the sermon's central theme from beginning to end is a major dynamic encouraging the listener's participation. Having once gotten on the bus the listeners now have a vested interest in where it is going and in when and how they will be getting off. Another part of maintaining their active involvement is, as Gardner Taylor has put it, always to preach with an exit lane in sight, that is, to be on the right road, headed in the right direction with a clear sense of when the trip is over, how to signal for the exit lane and how to stop the bus safely at the right place.

Here it is helpful to go back to the first naïve reading of the text and review the images and experiences and emotions evoked there that still seem now to be valid in relationship to the thematic statement arrived at as a result of the study process. Next, place these in order from those having the least to those having the most significance and emotional impact. A simple but important guideline in maintaining the interest of the listener's own heart and mind in what is being said is to consistently move from the less to the more significant emotional and evocative material. An old adage from the black preaching tradition captures this quite well: "Start low; go slow; go high, strike fire. Retire." This simple summary addresses the importance of movement within the sermon, the movement from lesser to greater evocative material, and the importance of knowing when to draw the sermon to a conclusion. Concerning this movement from less to greater emotional impact another adage from black preachers of an earlier generation again tells it simply and well: "Save a little gallop for the avenue." A good deal of potentially powerful material is often wasted because it is used to soon in the sermon. The ordering of material so as to use it for its best possible effect can help engage and sustain the hearts and minds of the listeners throughout the sermon, so that when its end is reached they will still be present, attentive, and responsive to it.

It is much better for the preacher to quit before she is finished than it is to go on too long after she has effectively done so. Having a carefully crafted sermon, ordering its emotional and affective as well as intellectual impact properly, is a healthy safeguard and helpful guideline in assuring, as best as can be done, that the sermon is finished neither before nor after it should be but rather where it ought to be. Such a sense of movement is important to the oral proclamation of the word. It calls, in part, on the emotional memory of both the preacher and the listener to sustain the sermon and move it forward. Preaching so formed is more than the dissemination of information. It is also the evocation of thought and memory and the creation of emotion, feeling, and aesthetic values. Preaching at its best and fullest is, in other words, both the giving of content and the giving of experience, so that the sermon speaks not so much to the people as it speaks for them, that is, on their behalf. When the listeners feel so involved it is highly likely that they will stay on the bus to the end of the line.

Garrison Keillor speaks of five elements needed to keep a good story moving: religion, money, family relationships, sex, and mystery. He then proceeds to put all five elements into one seventeen-word story: " 'Oh God,' the banker's daughter said, 'I'm pregnant and I don't even know who the father is!' "[7] Would that we preachers could be so succinct ourselves. I use Keillor's story here as a humorous but also fine example of the use of brevity and clarity in moving an idea along from start to finish.

Eugene Lowry, in his pioneering work on the sermon as narrative art form, has developed an insightful and helpful parallel between the movement of literary form and sermon structure.[8] He points out that there are two basic plot forms: the unknown conclusion, such as in the film classic *High Noon,* where a felt discrepancy moves toward an uncertain ending at the O.K. Corral; and the known conclusion, such as in the TV series *Columbo,* where the plot involves an unknown middle process, although the end is already known. In these, as in most narrative forms, the movement is from a felt discrepancy—an itch born of ambiguity—toward resolution or a release from the tension of that ambiguity. Most sermons tend to involve the second kind of plot, that is, the known conclusion. Christians already know that Abraham will not kill Isaac, that the Red Sea will part, that Easter follows Good Friday. The listeners expect to hear the gospel proclaimed that they, in fact, already know. The challenge for the preacher then becomes the same one Soren Kierkegaard faced in his native Denmark: How do you preach the Christian gospel in a Christian land? Or in more contemporary language, How do you preach to those who already know the tale and its ending? In applying literary form to sermon development, Lowry helps us see that it is the unknown middle ground that provides the context for the building of sermonic tension moving toward resolution for preachers today whose sermons are being delivered to listeners who know the story's ending as well as they themselves do. It is the movement from statement of the problem to its resolution that shapes the form of the sermon's own narrative in a way that engages the heart and the mind of the listeners as well as that of the preacher. This movement from felt discrepancy to resolution is what Lowry calls the homiletical plot. Following basic literary plot form and applying it to sermon development, he develops a five-stage plot sequence moving the sermon from discrepancy to resolution. These five stages are: (1) upsetting the equilibrium, (2) analyzing the discrepancy, (3) disclosing the clue to resolution, (4) experiencing the gospel, and (5) anticipating the consequences. Exercising some literary creativity himself he also describes the stages with these terms: (1) Oops; (2) Ugh; (3) Aha; (4) Whee;

and (5) Yeah.[9] These five stages are not to be conceived of as isolated parts of a whole but rather as stages of a forward-moving sequence, moving horizontally through the shared experience of preacher and listener rather than vertically as in the more static, didactic structure of a sermon outline in which the preacher is dispensing information to the listener.

Perhaps the most helpful way to demonstrate this five-stage narrative process, the movement from felt discrepancy to resolution of the discrepancy, is by showing its application in an actual sermon. The sermon that follows is one I preached at the congregation I've served since 1982 on the Seventh Sunday after the Epiphany in 1995. The text is the lectionary gospel lesson appointed for that Sunday, which is Luke 6:27-38. The sermon's title was "Love My Enemies?" and its summary thematic sentence was: Our inner response to life's pains and challenges is best determined neither by friends nor by enemies, but by God's faithfulness to us and by our faithfulness to God in Christ.

Each of the five stages of narrative development is indicated by the use of one of the summary terms *Oops, Ugh, Aha, Whee,* and *Yeah.*

## Stage One: "Oops"

Today's gospel lesson about loving and forgiving our enemies is difficult enough for people to hear who have only the normal range of hurts and irritations to deal with in their lives. How then might it be heard by victims of violent crimes and obvious injustices? Or, how might it be heard by aging German Lutherans now in their seventies and eighties gathering for worship in Dresden today, remembering the destruction of their city fifty years ago this week when three waves of British and U.S. bombers dropped nearly thirty-five hundred tons of explosives and phosphorous, igniting a firestorm that left the city in ashes and mourning over thirty-five thousand civilian war dead killed on February 13 or 14, 1945? I can see old women there today, standing in cemeteries, gazing at the graves of children who, had they lived, would now be in their fifties—those old women still weeping quietly, remembering, wondering "What if . . . ?" Bitterness is what I see in many of them. How easy is it for them to hear and to honor Jesus' counsel: "Love your enemies, do good to those who hate you, bless those who curse you, pray for those who abuse you" (Luke 6:27-28)? In our real and often harsh world this teaching of Jesus is not easy to accept or to honor through actual obedience. For many people it likely falls under the category of "Things I wish Jesus had never said." But of course, he did, and so they are there for us to deal with as best we can.

## Stage Two: "Ugh"

Jesus is describing here, in the Sermon on the Plain in Luke's Gospel, what only he himself can fully attain. But in describing this behavior he also is describing the future that God is calling us to, as well as describing a way to live more fully in the present, not bound by bitterness, hatred, and fear, because whenever we are bound by such things we may be aggressive, we may even be dominant, but we are not free. In a recent newspaper article, for instance, I read about a Jewish settler who read psalms at the tomb of Baruch Goldstein, who is considered a saint in that Jewish settlement because he had killed twenty-nine Muslim worshipers in Hebron in 1994 and was then himself beaten to death.

Are either that Jewish settler or the Muslim worshipers who killed Goldstein free? Or are those understandably embittered students at Rutgers University, enraged by President Francis Lawrence's recent remarks about the possibility of genetic deficiencies in black members of the student body, free? On both the West Bank and the university campus the bitterness is real and understandable, but it is also destructive and self-perpetuating. It is only a matter of time until more Muslims or Jews are killed, until other disturbances linked to racial bigotry and oppression erupt. The long, sad story of Northern Ireland weaves the same tale, as do so many untold stories of private bitterness and rage at injustice and senseless loss that deeply touch so many hearts and memories.

How hard this teaching of Jesus is to honor when we see it so concretely related to actual lived experience. "Love your enemies, do good to those who hate you, bless those who curse you, pray for those who abuse you."

Could you do that? Do you do it? This teaching surely qualifies as one of what scholars have called the "hard sayings" of Jesus.

## Stage Three: "Aha"

But we are not totally without hope in this matter because there are those who have responded to evil with freedom and in doing so have shown us the way to a different possibility. Joseph in today's Old Testament Lesson, turning his brothers' intended evil into good, is one of them. The key to such a resolution lies first in the grace and power of God and then also in our awareness of the possibility of choice in response to the evil we may encounter. Such possibility of choice in response to evil is told in the story of Victor Frankl, who was an abused prisoner of war during World War II. He suffered severe torture and innumerable unspeakable violations of his body. But one day, left naked and alone for a moment in a small room, he began to become aware of what he was later to call "the last of the human freedoms," the one his captors could neither control nor take away from him. They could and they did do whatever they wanted to do to his body and his environment, but they could not touch his soul: the inner man, his God-given identity. He realized that he was still free to decide, within himself, how all of this was going to affect him and that between the evil that happened to him and his response to it was his God-given freedom—his power to choose that response. In that moment he became a free man again, although he endured much more torture and pain before the war ended and he was freed. Some twenty-five years ago I heard him tell his story in person, and although he is Jewish, I heard a profoundly hopeful gospel word coming from him that moved me then and still moves me deeply: God has so made us that we can endure any loss and any evil so long as we have an inner sense of our freedom to choose our response to it.

## Stage Four: "Whee"

As Christians our own foundational story is about someone who did this very thing. Jesus, at Calvary, experienced the direct, overwhelming stimulus of the cross with all its attendant shame and pain, its rejection and ridicule—all the forces of evil gathered around the very one against whom they had no honest claim. Yet there on that hill, where the world had lost its equilibrium on that Good Friday, Jesus experienced this same sense of inner freedom between the stimulus of the cross and his response to it. And in that freedom, there in the face of all the gathered forces of evil, he chose forgiveness, compassion, courage, love, and finally submission to this father's will.

In doing so he did not allow the evil he experienced to define him, rather he chose to define himself in the inner freedom that was his even there on the cross. Who was truly free there that stark holy day? Those who walked smugly away, unharmed? Or the one who, left there hanging bound on the cross, was free to forgive them?

## Stage Five: "Yeah"

We too are free to choose our "inner response" to any evil or injustice we may know—to define ourselves from the inside and not solely from our exterior circumstances or by what others around us do to us. We too are free to choose, and in that precious defining freedom is lodged both our responsibility to act and our own potential for growth and healing.

May such freedom heal and free the bound hearts of Germans remembering Dresden today, of Palestinians and Jews, of abused spouses and children, of the victims of crime and violence, and of any of us present who are now bound by some remembered injustice, some painful violation, some bitter memory, and thus neither whole nor free ourselves, so that the love of even our enemies may lead us all to God's intended healing and salvation. It is not an easy road to travel, but it leads to freedom. Thanks be to God. Amen.

This sermon was an attempt to move from felt discrepancy (Oops) through resolution (Yeah), using each of the five stages of homiletical plot form. A primary value of this form is its sustained sense of tension moving toward release and resolution. Rather than developing logically from point to point, it develops sequentially from stage to stage. The narrative plot form has a sense of horizontal rather than vertical direction, of moving through time rather than space. It often is more conversational than instructional in tone and its focus is much more on engaging and evoking response than it is on tamping in information. It often also expresses its truth in an indirect, or as Emily Dickinson would have put it, a "slanted" way, rather than as direct didactic discourse. In form it is related more to the short story than to the lecture. It attempts to establish a meaningful level of identity with the listener, and it uses image and story and metaphor more than precise, distinction-making language to communicate its message and express its truth. And it attempts to leave room for the listener's own response.

Clarifying the message of the text is the function of the study method outlined above. Attempting to develop the most open and sustainable hearing of that message is the function of the movement of the message in the experience of the listener. And communicating that message through the evocative images of metaphor and story is the function of the language the preacher uses in attempting to address both the mind and the heart of the listener. It is to the valuing and development of such language we now turn.

## Speaking the Text: Metaphor

What language ought we preachers use to tell the most precious story we know to the dear, vulnerable people to whom we preach and with whom we also stand under the same sentence of death—the final sign of our common mortality—and with all of us knowing it? What language is strong enough and tender enough to help us speak with honesty, courage, and strength as "a dying man to dying men," as we've already heard the seventeenth-century divine Richard Baxter, with compelling clarity, describe the earnestness of his own preaching? Or, as John Ruskin once described the importance of the preaching ministry, it is that hour when men and women come in, breathless and weary with the week's labor, and a man "sent with a message," which is a matter of life and death, has but thirty minutes to get at the separate hearts . . . to convince them of all their weaknesses . . . to try by this way and that to stir the hard fastenings of those doors . . . thirty minutes to raise the dead in!—let us but once understand and feel this, and the pulpit will become a throne, like unto a marble rock in the desert, about which the people gather to slake their thirst.[10]

Given this high view of the prophetic and pastoral ministry of the preaching office, what language is worthy of the endeavor to speak in such a way? The strongest, most tender language I know for this high privilege is the language of metaphor. It is to its consideration that we now turn.

Cardinal Newman is said to have observed that the all-wise, all-knowing God cannot speak without meaning many things at once. Here I think he was describing part of the richness of metaphor, which evokes levels of meaning, each of which bears its own truth, from a single image. Things can be "true" for us in different ways, although in our own contentious time this is becoming less and less an accepted reality. It is being replaced by "my" reality becoming "the" reality. Biblical scholar Marcus Borg has pointed out that while conservatives "insist that everything in the Bible must be factual in order to be true," their more liberal counterparts

seek to rescue a few facts from the fire. Both camps seem largely unaware that we live in the only culture in human history that has equated truth with factuality. This has had a pernicious effect on our ability to appreciate the Bible, with its interweaving of history and metaphor and symbolic narrative.[11]

At the outset, then, it is clear that there is both resistance to and confusion about the language of metaphor. Yet ironically its use is pervasive even among its most ardent resisters—the popularity of Hallmark anniversary and birthday greeting cards being a simple, obvious case in point: "Love is a golden bond," "The years pass as a sweet river's flow," and so forth.

It is incumbent upon preachers to recover the richness of the language of metaphor because even with all of its ambiguities and levels of meaning it still is the sweetest, most effective and powerful language we preachers have to tell the most important story we have to tell. It also bears the most promise of evoking the deepest, fullest response of our listeners to that story as well.

In a discussion of "myths" concerning the Virgin Mary, Kathleen Norris says, "By 'myth' I mean a story that you know must be true the first time you hear it. Or, in the words of a five-year-old child, as related by Gertrud Mueller Nelson in her recent Jungian interpretation of fairy tales and Marian theology, *Here All Dwell Free*, a myth is a story that isn't true on the outside, only on the inside."[12] Norris goes on to say that "human beings . . . require myth as one of the basic necessities of life" and that "once we have our air and water and a bit of food, we turn [whether we call it so or not] to metaphor and to myth-making."[13]

Metaphor is valuable language for preachers precisely because it is not vapid. It has it grounding in the five senses and draws on images from the natural world rather than on blank terms such as *reality,* which is a popular word among preachers but one having no grounding in actual human experience at all. It is much better to describe a particular reality—fire, water, wind, terror, laughter, tears, than it is to speak of reality in general. There is no reality in general, just as there is no human life in general either. Life is specific, physical, locatable in time and space, and so ought our language describing it be. The Incarnation is, after all, the ultimate metaphor—God's own wondrous, unfathomable design yoking the human and the divine. Whenever our own "God-talk" is speech that seems unaware of this mystery, it becomes a false language, eloquent perhaps, but lacking in grace and power to speak a good word to the wounded hearts and weary minds who gather in church faithfully, week after week, hoping yet again to hear such a word spoken.

Eugene Peterson has suggested that the theologian's best ally is the artist, because church leaders should be passionately interested in how the creative process works—not in how to say things accurately. He goes on to say that communicating clearly is not primarily what we are after. What we are after, rather, is creating new life and possibility. Poets and creative writers are interested not in saying things as accurately as possible but in touching the human heart and in letting the human imagination work in creative, analogical ways. Of the use of language in preaching Peterson says, "We have such a fear of superstition and allegory that we squeezed all the imaginative stuff out of Scripture so we could be sure that it was just precise and accurate. If it's the infallible Word, well then you've got to have the exact meaning and nothing else, so all ambiguity goes. Well, all good language is ambiguous. It's poetic. It has levels of meaning, so which one of those levels of meaning is infallible?"[14]

Metaphor is the basis of all language and thought, just as it is of all religion. The very origin of language is most likely rooted in a metaphorical enterprise. As Thomas Cahill points out, language probably began "in the human attempt to mimic certain sounds, so that, for instance, the sound 'ma-ma,' a form of which all languages use for 'mother,' began as an imitation of the sucking sound a baby makes at the breast. Deep within each of us, the need for correspondence remains. . . . This is why something inside us responds spontaneously to metaphor, the heart of all poetry and finally, of all language and all meaning."[15] Metaphor is simply the language of our basic human experience, a language that also touches the soul. Could there be a better language for the preacher to use?

The most appropriate language for the preacher is that which speaks both to her own mind and heart and to the mind and heart of the listener. This thought was well-known, for instance, to novelist Saul Bellow, whose earlier quoted comment in *Humboldt's Gift* is especially apt here again. "By themselves abstractions will not travel. They must pass through the heart to be transmitted."[16] That thought is one that has informed my own preparation for preaching for many years. It offers an apt reminder to us preachers of the kind of process that nurtures the possibility of evoking new correspondences, new insights, new life within us and thus through us also within those to whom we will preach.

But, how do we best get there? I believe that the best route is not the circumscribed one of lecture, logic, and analytical thought, although these all have their proper place in church and in society. The more promising route, rather, is the more circuitous one of metaphor, image, and story. The gospel is itself, after all, not a creedal statement but a story. Jesus himself gave us his most memorable teaching in these very forms: the good Samaritan, the prodigal son, faith like a mustard seed, sheep on a hillside. Here are enduring truths hidden in images and metaphors and stories. And when the New Testament writers themselves attempt to define or describe the single word *Jesus,* they use many different images to do so. Among these images are: Redeemer, Savior, Emmanuel, Messiah, Long-Expected One, King of kings, Prince of Peace—all of them, synonyms for the one single name Jesus. And there are many more, no less than twenty-five lines of such entries in one thesaurus alone. The list of these metaphors testifies to the complexity and depth of faith that stands behind them: Star of David, Good Shepherd, Bright Morning Star, Healer, Door, Way, Bread of Life, Cup of Salvation, Truth, Light. Which of these is Jesus? All of them and many more. The power and beauty of metaphor is its ability to release the imagination, to evoke from our own deepest inner places images that ring true for us and that touch our hearts as well as our minds.

One way to speak our truth is through the precise, distinction-making, formalistic language of systematic theology, and great Christian thinkers have always done so to the clear advantage of the church and the church's understanding of its faith and its mission. This is not, however, how Jesus himself spoke when he trusted that the truth of divine instruction would best be carried to the hearts and minds of his listeners through the words and images of simple parable and tale. And didn't it work quite well? Most church-going Christians could come reasonably close to retelling the parables of the prodigal son or the good Samaritan and also have a pretty solid grasp of their intended meaning. And there isn't a single argumentative polemical or doctrinal word in either of them. It is metaphor, not polemic, that allows Jesus to describe the kingdom of God in terms of mustard seed and yeast and its presence within us. Similarly it is metaphor that now allows us preachers and our listeners too, at some perhaps inarticulate but felt level, to "get it" without having to have it neatly packaged and explained all the time.

The nineteenth-century mathematician and inventor of differential equations Bernhard Riemann said of his work that he did not invent those pairs of differential equations—he only found them in the world where God had hidden them. What humility, insight, humor, wisdom, and grace stand behind Riemann's words. And yet, however, did God literally go around hiding differential equations in hard-to-find places on the earth in order to make life difficult for theoretical mathematicians? Not likely. But, does that also mean there is no truth in Riemann's observation? No, it certainly doesn't. In fact, to me his comment makes the exploration of differential equations (about which I know nothing) much more appealing and intelligible. Here again the passage from George MacDonald's *Ranald Bannerman's Boyhood* seems fitting: "It is not necessary that the intellect should define and separate before the heart and soul derive nourishment. As well say that a bee can get nothing out of a flower, because she does not understand botany. . . . The best influences which bear upon us are of this vague sort—powerful upon the heart and conscience, although undefined to the intellect."[17] This kind of openness to new possibilities of knowing through language can nurture and honor the presence of wonder and beauty and grace in each of us preachers as we dare to speak and in each of our listeners as they dare to listen.

Barbara Brown Taylor, in a passage in *The Preaching Life*, says that "the church's central task is an imaginative one," by which she means not "a fanciful or fictional task, but one in which the human capacity to imagine," to form new hopeful images of self and neighbor and world and work and the future, "is both engaged and transformed." She says, further, that children are "virtuosi" at imagination and that they can be our teachers. They are the ones still able to "drape towels over their shoulders and become monarchs in ermine cloaks with toilet brush scepters."[18] Their lives are enriched and graced by metaphor at nearly every turn. "Part of their secret," Taylor says, "is their natural ability to employ all their senses. . . . Their other advantage is their ignorance of adult notions of what things are supposed to be and do. Adults may agree that a comb is for combing hair, but children . . . know that a comb is also a musical instrument, a sifter for seashells hidden in the sand, a back scratcher for dogs, and a tool for making racetracks for ants. . . . To apprentice oneself to a child is to learn that the world is full of wonders."[19] It is also to learn that the world is full of graceful, life-renewing metaphors. As Gail Ramshaw has expressed it, "Metaphor is the vehicle for repositioning old boundaries and for proposing new insight."[20] Or, as Paul Ricoeur has said, metaphor is "the birthing room of meaning."[21] A further example of the richness of metaphor comes from the black preaching tradition, where instead of a direct reference to the sun's movement, the preacher might say: "I looked and saw the first thin pencil line of dawn, and watched God's ball of fire seek its noon meridian, continue its relentless journey to the twilight and then lay down to sleep beyond the western hills."[22]

Of the following two ways of describing the person of Jesus, (1) "the incarnational reality constituent of the Second Person of the Holy Trinity," or (2) "the Bright Morning Star," I hope that the preacher at the funeral of someone very dear to me, or at my own funeral, spoken to someone grieving me, has enough compassion and enough sense of the evocative and healing power of metaphor to speak of the One in whom our final trust is placed and to whom we are all finally entrusted as the Bright Morning Star who will guide us all safely home.

# 5

# COMMUNICATING THE HEAD AND HEART CONNECTION EFFECTIVELY

℘

Since I am coming to that holy room,
   where, with thy choir of saints for evermore,
I shall be made thy music; as I come
   I tune the instrument here at the door,
   and what I must do then, think here before.

JOHN DONNE
"A Hymne to God, My God in My Sicknesse"

## The Importance of "How"

The mystery of the preaching office is clearly and simply expressed in the Confessio Helvetica Posterior: *Praedicatio verbi dei est verbum dei,* that is, the congregation believes it encounters the presence of God in the words of the preacher. In such an understanding the sermon acquires a near sacramental quality, that is, it speaks of the real presence of God residing in the spoken words of the preacher.[1] Rudolf Bultmann is among the theologians who have emphasized this view. Although Karl Barth didn't go quite so far, even he characterized the sermon as a "salvation event." Barth recognized that just as in the sacraments, so too in preaching something is dispensed in the proclamation of the word: God gives of Godself. Or, as the bracing words of scripture itself express it, "Whoever speaks must do so as one speaking the very words of God . . . so that God may be glorified in all things through Jesus Christ" (1 Peter 4:11). Given such a high view of the importance of the spoken word it is only prudent and faithful stewardship for the preacher to be concerned with how that word can most effectively be spoken. Our attention turns in this chapter, then, to the theologically significant and pragmatically focused "how" of the dynamic preaching event engaging both the preacher and the listener.

*Hermeneutics* is a term literally meaning to draw out what is inside. In the contemporary field of seminary education and biblical studies it is used to convey a method of interpreting the scriptures. The hermeneutic of the early monastic tradition, by contrast, was much simpler. A younger monk would approach one of his elders with the request "Speak a word, Father," which once having received, the younger monk would attempt to put into practice in his own daily life.[2] In this chapter we will consider the importance of the words we preachers speak and how best to speak them. In doing so we may perhaps also learn to bring honor to the ancient request of the searcher's heart—often unspoken but felt yet in our listener's heart today—"Speak a word, Father."

The "how" question is not, after all, an unimportant

one for the preacher, although it often has taken a back seat to questions of "what" and "why" in academic circles. In the sanctuary this ought not be the case. Clear communication is difficult and the question of how to communicate to others the most important story the preacher has to tell is an important matter for both preacher and listener. How to overcome the distance between them remains a central concern for effective preaching today. Such effective preaching is rooted in the ability to establish a relationship among three elements: preacher, listener, and sermon. A part of the preacher's task is to encourage and enable the listeners to participate meaningfully in this relationship. The principles of communication presented here under the headings *Partnering, Action, Freeing the Text, Listening, Speaking,* and *Scripting* are intended to aid the preacher in the realization of that goal.[3]

## Principles of Effective Communication

### Partnering

John Woolman's journal reports a conversation between Woolman and an old Native American, Chief Papunehang, in which he says, "I have to feel where words come from."[4] Such an inner sense for words is also an important part of the dynamic between preacher and listener in the partnership involved in preaching. A central challenge for the preacher is how to get his partners "out there" to become engaged with the sermon as their own experience and not only the experience of the preacher. What is done in preaching ought to be done in order to evoke a response of engagement from the listeners in building a relationship with the preacher, the sermon, and themselves. An essential part of every sermon delivered, every lesson read, every

**115**

prayer offered in worship has to do with the engagement of the partner. In order to accomplish this the preacher must be authentically interested in his listeners as partners in worship and also curious about and responsive to them. The preacher needs to know what it means to have partners in the preaching event and to engage those partners actively in it.

At its best, a sermon is something that is done together, so that some of the responsibility, some of the energy, some of the resources for it are out there with the partners and not all in the pulpit with the preacher. This can be a freeing thought for the preacher personally as well as a freeing conceptual approach to the preaching event. The preacher's partners have some responsibility too. By being curious about them and responsive to them the preacher can help them realize that they do. The key is not to do all of the work for them. It's all right to leave some questions unanswered, a few stones unturned in the gardens of their minds. The preacher's partners do have some responsibility to till their own soil. The key is the distinction between giving the partners a neat, tightly packaged message and getting them engaged in searching for meaning themselves. The sermon should help open the text for the partners and not simply "tell them" what it "means." The Bible is not the preacher's book. It is the church's book. The preacher's partners, then, can and should think about and respond to its messages themselves—not without thoughtful guidance, of course, but also not through ministerial coercion. Too often we preachers seem to think that we need to be "answer people." This is an unreasonable and unnecessary self-imposed burden. It also makes it more difficult for us to be truly curious about other people in a nonmanipulative way. This is significant both theologically and pastorally because, in large measure, it is curiosity that encourages humanity. When you are authentically curious about another person, you become much more interested in evoking a response than in manipulating or determining it. The preacher's task is not to determine the partner's response to the gospel's message but to free that message in the partner's presence so that the partner can respond to it.

Partnering in preaching can lead to a deeper awareness of the presence, worth, and contribution of persons other than the preacher in the preaching event. It is also an expression of sincere desire to be in touch with and curious about other people and a way of nurturing an openness to and a valuing of their contribution to the preacher's life and the richness they bring, as partners, to the preaching event. The principle of partnering in preaching is really a way of life, not a technique to be used to look good or to "win" others to one's own point of view. It is in daily living that we preachers too can learn to value being curious about and open to others—valuing them as partners on our spiritual pilgrimage. This, in turn, can nurture and develop a depth and fullness in both the preaching office and the pastoral ministry that they might otherwise not have. In order to glean the most possibility from the learnings of such curiosity and partnering, one thing must be yielded: the need to be the expert answer person at all times. The benefits of mutual growth in faith and encouragement in life, however, far outweigh this limitation. As R. E. C. Browne once astutely observed, "To hear a minister of the Word preach often should not be to know him better but to know yourself better and only to increase in your knowledge of him through what you realize he has shown you about yourself." Sermons are true partnerships "when each listener feels that as a result of the sermon he understands himself better and sees more clearly the individual response that the Gospel demands from him."[5] Such partnerships involving preacher, listener, and sermon are not always comfortable, but they can become profoundly meaningful.

## Action

Preaching is commonly thought of and practiced by many as a literary endeavor, but it really is no such thing. Our educational system is dominated by print. In it we have become primarily visually oriented, dominated by the written and read word. Preaching, however, is much more an art of the ear than of the eye and sermons belong to the art of the spoken word, not to the art of the written word. As J. Phillip Swander characterized it, "Preaching is a special and distinct art form. It asks of us that we recognize its nature, restore to it its integrity."[6] At the heart of preaching—its fundamental element—is action, that is, preaching is an art of the spoken word, an art of action, of doing, and not simply one of thinking and reading aloud words off a page.

Any spoken communication involves more than words. It is also, and primarily, an action. Something is happening whenever words are spoken and heard. Understanding preaching as an action more than as the transmission of thought is a significant step toward understanding what is at the heart of it. Action is the fundamental principle of communication. The most gifted stage actors understand this to be the bedrock principle of their art. The very word *drama* derives from a Greek word that means "deed." Its verb form translates as "to do, to act," that is, to do something— not to "play-act" or to become theatrical in the pulpit—but rather to be aware of what it is one is "doing" there.[7]

The basic question in communication is "What are you doing?" and not "What are you saying?" Words alone cannot possibly contain the whole of any spoken message. The message, rather, is in the doing of it, which involves the words, the sounds, the body, the voice, the gestures, the inflection, the pace, the posture, the intention, the intensity, the passion, that is, the whole being of the person through whom the message is being communicated. It isn't just the preacher's head that is in the pulpit come Sunday morning. It is the preacher's whole being, all that he is, all that he has been, all that he has done or failed to do, all that he can yet become that is present there. Whether hesitant or eager to communicate, what will be communicated is much more than the words that will be spoken.

The best way to communicate an action is to do it, not to explain it. To get a sense of this principle try the following exercise, devised by Phillip Swander, aloud. Simply say the single word, *hello,* in such a way as to communicate these various meanings: "Why fancy meeting you here!" (Surprise); "You finally got here, I see." (Irritation); "I don't care if you're here or not." (Indifference); or "What the devil are you doing here?" (Anger).[8] Doing such a simple exercise can begin to help establish the connection between the spoken word and the action behind it. This is an important connection for preachers to understand because words don't carry themselves in preaching. It is the action behind and beyond the words that carries them, which is why it is important for the preacher to know what he is doing when preaching and not just what he is saying.

Another Swander exercise may help clarify the important connection between the words spoken in sermons and the actions behind them. The focus of the exercise is on demonstrating how the same words can communicate messages that are quite different from one another. If, for instance, the intended action behind the words *I love you* is "to embrace," the listeners will hear one thing. But if the action behind those same words is "to despair," then the listeners will hear something else. Swander's third column, the "ad lib" column, introduces a way of hearing "in the mind's ear" the tone of the action the speaker wishes to communicate.

| ACTION | WORDS SPOKEN | THE "AD LIB" |
|---|---|---|
| To Embrace | I love you | (I'm glad.) |
| To Fish for | I love you | (Do you love me?) |
| To Protest | I love you | (Are you deaf, dumb, and blind?!) |
| To Insist | I love you | (Whatever you may think!) |
| To Revel | I love you | (I'm in heaven.) |
| To Lust | I love you | (Hot d__n!) |
| To Despair | I love you | (I wish I didn't!) |
| To Give in | I love you | (There's nothing I can do about it.)[9] |

This exercise demonstrates how knowing the action determines how the words are felt, spoken or sounded, that is, how they are communicated to the listener. The words are exactly the same. It is the meaning that changes and yet is clear. As Swander counsels, "To speak is to act. You cannot speak and not do something. It is, therefore, foolhardy and dangerous to speak and not know what you are doing."[10]

In a sermon that engages the listener everything flows from its action and is carried along by its movement much more than by its ideas. There is no real momentum to a sermon unless the preacher's partners are engaged. And the preacher's "reflections" or "observations" or "five points about . . . " won't carry them very far. But, if the actions of the sermon are such as the listeners can respond to, they'll come along. Most people like to be where the action is, or at least understand what it's about. The essential ingredient in evocative, engaging preaching, its fundamental element, is action.

## Freeing the Text

The sermon is not the only thing the preacher speaks aloud during the worship service. In most typical worship settings the preacher also reads aloud the text for the sermon that is to follow. The speaking and hearing of that text plays an important role in building the nest into which the egg of the sermon is soon to be placed. Ideally the listeners should "overhear" the preacher speaking the text to them and listening to the text himself. The goal is to help the listeners discover the meaning of the text for themselves, not to pack the preacher's understanding of it into them from the outside. To "speak" a biblical text faithfully is first of all to "give ear" to it oneself, then to be aware that other people are overhearing what is being spoken and are also listening to the preacher listen to the text as well. It may seem a bit unusual to say that the preacher needs to listen to himself as he speaks but that is just what is meant. The more the preacher is genuinely able to listen to the text as he is speaking it, the less he will have to do for the listeners, that is, the less he will have to impose his own emotional responses and interpretations on the text, thereby subtly limiting the listeners' responses to the limits of the preacher's vision. The purpose of speaking the text aloud in worship ought not be to instruct or

121

limit others as to how they should understand it, but rather, insofar as possible, to set it free in their lives. To accomplish this it is important not to get in the way of the text by trying to dramatize it with staged inflections, pauses, and points of emphasis. If the preacher is listening for what is happening in the text—for its action—as it is being spoken, then he will soon discover that it will find its own voice, through his voice, into the listening ears and waiting hearts of his partners.

All of this is to suggest that the preacher respect and honor the voice of the text. It has a life and an integrity of its own. It was here long before any of us preachers arrived and it will be here long after we are gone. It doesn't need yet another flashy rendition. It has suffered through and survived too many of those already. The preacher simply needs to listen to the text as he speaks it and gives it voice. The way the words have lived in it already now for two thousand years and more is a large part of its meaning. The preacher doesn't need to create that meaning but rather needs simply to release it.

Practically speaking, punctuation marks in biblical texts are for grammatical purposes and for silent reading and not necessarily for places where pauses should be placed while speaking aloud. For both pace and meaning, for instance, it is frequently more appropriate to read through commas than it is to pause at them. The syntax of the sentences themselves is the best single guideline in this regard. Most of the active listening of the preacher's partners takes place while the preacher is actually speaking and not in the silences and pauses. So it is important for the preacher also to be listening even while speaking. Being consciously aware that active listening is going on while the preacher is speaking can help the preacher pace the silences and pauses and points of emphasis in a more helpful, less controlling, more evenly balanced way. Pacing becomes less contrived and burdensome and more natural, engaging and alive whenever the preacher himself also listens as he speaks.

Speaking biblical texts aloud faithfully and well is no easy thing. Especially if the preacher is good at speaking and has a pleasant or commanding voice, the temptation to be impressive is great and easily enough succumbed to. The strongest defense against such temptation is to listen to the text first of all as a believer oneself, to stand under its authority, to hear its wisdom, to be led by its guidance, to respond to its grace. The text is much older and stronger and wiser than anyone whose privilege it is to give it voice on Sunday morning. We preachers are not the text's masters; we are its servants. Wonder, awe, humility, awareness, curiosity, restraint, and a good listening ear are all needed for effective, faithful releasing of the text within the hearing of the people gathered for worship. The preacher is the instrument of the text's release. When it is spoken it, not the speaker of it, ought to be the focus of the listener's attention. There is something humbling in that. But then again perhaps there ought to be.

## Listening

An effective preacher must also be an active listener in the pulpit. It is simply an incomplete communication if the speaker does not show evidence of interest in the responses of the listeners to what is being said and done. The question for the speaker always to keep in mind in relationship to the listeners is "What do they think about this?" Such curiosity about the listening partners in preaching sends a clear message to them that they are both involved and valued as participants in the sermon, which at its best isn't just the preacher talking but also the people listening and responding.

The minute the preacher no longer has a partner he starts to "preach," and in this instance that is not intended as a compliment. Whenever we preachers are really curious about our listening partners we won't "perform" in the pulpit. Our focus won't be on ourselves but on our listeners, with an authentic curiosity about their involvement and an active listening for their responses. However, such listening doesn't carry with it the expectation that someone literally will respond aloud to each of the sermon's statements with comments like, "Hey now that's an interesting idea!" or "I don't agree with you on that point." Listening while preaching is, rather, an inner attitude of openness and curiosity that acknowledges and values the presence of others in the preaching event and is a way of indicating their importance to it. In other words, listening to one's preaching partners is not a gimmick or a technique; it is a pastoral disposition of the heart toward and about them. Such interest is not necessarily demonstrated by the use of an intentional well-placed dramatic pause. Often such pauses draw more attention to the preacher than to the listener. But, if the preacher is listening for the unspoken responses of the listeners, curious about how they are engaged with the sermon and responding to it, then his pauses will be authentic and natural. Their length and frequency is not nearly as important as their appropriateness. It is also important not to "playact" at listening, giving the appearance of listening with no real substance behind it. Such playacting calls attention to the preacher in an undesirable way. In contrast, careful listening calls attention to the preacher's partners in an encouraging, desirable way. The best way I know to get listeners interested is to be interested in them.

124

Listening is, in the final analysis, a matter of character. It is a matter of valuing the life and dignity of every fellow child of God as much as you do your own. A part of that valuing is to be present to them with full attention when you are in their presence and to be curious about their lives, their joys, and their sorrows and about how things are between them and their God. Listening is a matter of character because it removes the self from the center and places God there, where God in mercy stands in loving relationship to preacher and listener alike. Such an understanding of listening is really a spiritual discipline, a way of life that takes incarnational faith seriously. Because God is present in the lives of both preachers and their listening partners, all of those lives are precious and blessed and eternally significant. The preacher's faithful, pastoral listening strengthens the bonds of nurture and love, takes incarnational faith seriously, and opens channels for powerful and effective communication of the gospel.

## Speaking

As the primary leader of worship, the pastor speaks in various roles. His roles include liturgist, lector, preacher, and intercessor. The suggestions presented here are intended to offer practical guidance as well as theological perspective on speaking in these various worship contexts.

The first point to be noted is that it is a reverence for words that ought to lead to their disciplined, thoughtful use in liturgy, sermon, and prayer. It is because words are so important and precious that there needs to be both restraint and economy in their use in worship. Because words are so powerful they can be both helpful and hurtful, both disturbing and comforting. They thus need to be treated with respect when they are spoken or read. They don't just represent thoughts. They are, in themselves, deeds. They do something to those in whose presence they are spoken. Consider, for instance, the single word "Fire!" shouted in a dark and crowded theater, or the word "Duck!" shouted when a dangerous instrument is flying though the air in your direction. An economy of words, yes. But not lacking in either purpose, meaning, or power. Spoken words have their own authority and importance. They perform their own actions when released into the life of the gathered community. Preparing to speak and read them thoughtfully and well is a faithful pastoral ministry. The world's best ballerinas and divas have been found "at the bar" or practicing their scales on the morning following the best performance of their lives. We preachers have been entrusted with communicating the word of God to others, with being its voice in our communities of faith. Ought not we be at least as disciplined by our art?

The words that we preachers read or speak in worship services are symbols that point toward experiences people have had or long yet to have with the holy. To read or speak those words armed with that knowledge can help keep us from glibness in their use. Such an awareness of what we are doing doesn't need to preclude the presence of joy but it surely does preclude the presence of cuteness and of handling the holy things of God too lightly. When we know what it is we are doing and saying and in whose presence it is being done and said, we will not, in all likelihood, be glib.

In practical terms, when reading or speaking aloud in worship, try to imagine reading or speaking these words as though they are being heard, by both the speaker and the listeners, for the first time, even though they've likely been heard many times before. If the speaker listens while speaking and attempts to speak with the focus, concentration, and clarity required of a first reading, then those words, spoken or read, have a life and vitality that isn't forced but flows naturally from an earnest desire to communicate any new and important information. For example, I remember reading once about a famous Scottish preacher who, while preparing for an Easter sermon, was reading the resurrection narratives in the gospels. It suddenly occurred to him that Jesus really was alive. He then reports having said, "I couldn't wait to tell my people!" Reading the old and familiar texts of the Bible, leading the well-known liturgy, reading from the lectern, speaking from the pulpit, or praying from the altar as though for the first time has this kind of response as its goal, for both preacher and listener alike.

Communicating through reading or speaking is more than communicating information; it is communicating meaning. It is a high privilege and great responsibility for pastors to speak and to read in worship. Reading and speaking to others in such a setting is a conduit for an encounter with the holy otherness of the sovereign God made known to us most fully in the words and deeds of Jesus Christ. Long ago Augustine understood that being in such a place isn't always either comforting or comfortable when he said that those who stand near the Christ stand near the fire. Being called as ministers of the gospel to lead and to speak in the public worship services of the church places us preachers very near that sacred fire. It is only prudent and wise that whenever we speak there we consider well what it is we are saying and why and how we are saying it.

## Scripting

A perennial debate among preachers and teachers of preaching centers on the use of a "manuscript" in preaching. There are well-reasoned arguments as well as good practitioners on various sides of this debate. Here I want simply to take a practical approach and assume that most preachers carry something with them into the pulpit besides the Bible and their anxiety. I want to look briefly at what that something might be in best aiding the preacher to make the connection between head and heart in himself and in his listeners.

For some preachers that "something" is a full manuscript. For others it is a detailed outline. For yet others it is a few words or images jotted on a page as a memory device. Whatever it is, it should not stand between the preacher and the listener but rather be an aid in the facilitation of effective communication. More creative energy needs to be spent by and among us preachers in learning how to be freed *by* our "manuscripts," whatever form they may take, rather than *from* them.

*Sermon* and *writing* aren't words that naturally go together like *book* and *writing* do. Sermons are intended for an oral/aural world, so that *speaking* and *listening* are words that go together more naturally in preaching than *speaking* and *writing* do. Yet, if most preachers do, in fact, use some sort of written material in the pulpit, what type of material might best serve to help the preacher make the head and heart connection most effectively? J. Phillip Swander used the word *scripting* to describe a process for what needs to be done and can be most helpful and freeing for preachers who feel the need to carry something with them into the pulpit.[11]

Swander argued that writing sermons places them first of all on paper, from which they then have to be taken in order to be communicated. This simply adds another step to an already demanding process because it means that the sermon now needs to be lifted off the written page and into the realm of oral/aural communication. What is written in manuscript form often is more appropriate for reading than for speaking. It is linear and conceptual, prepared with the mind of the partner in view, not the ear. Yet, in its final form it will be presented and received in an oral/aural form, that is, one will speak it and others will hear it. The voice and the ear are the primary physical means of communicating the sermon, not the eye. This is, in part, what makes the use of a manuscript such hard work. The sermon doesn't reside on the printed manuscript page but in the dynamic exchange connecting the heart and mind of the preacher to the hearts and minds of the listeners in the speaking and hearing of the sermon.

Some of the most noted American preachers have used full manuscripts in their preaching and have done so to great and lasting effect. They have a gift for this and are not bound by their printed words but are able to use this form to speak clearly and freely. Many other preachers who use this form, however, are not able to do so nearly as freely. For them, scripting may be a much more effective way to utilize the clarifying discipline of writing in preparing for sermon delivery than either full manuscript or outline preparation might provide, because scripting can help the preacher intentionally prepare for the sermon with an oral/aural world in view. Scripting can allow for the "doing" of the sermon—for its action—in a way that neither a full manuscript nor an outline can do in quite the same way. For example, when looking at a scripted page the eye would see, insofar as possible, what it is the speaker wants to hear himself say. In other words, there may be no consecutively written sentences or even sub-points of an outline on a given page at all. Instead there may be six words of increasing printed size or a listing of descriptive words or names moving upward from the lower left-hand corner of the page to the upper right-hand corner, perhaps with a smiley face or other visual cue sitting at the top. The point is to use the script to help establish and maintain contact with the partners through the ears, both the preacher's ears and the partner's ears. Listening to them is much more important than, for instance, remembering to establish "eye contact" with as many of them as possible. Establishing eye contact can easily become just another technique, like the forced pause, lacking both integrity and helpful effect. Sometimes eye contact is more akin to staring than it is to honest curiosity or the desire to establish authentic communication. Most people become uncomfortable when they are stared at, especially if the staring is being done by an authority figure. Their general response is to divert their own gaze along with their attention. Winning such a blinking contest ought not be the preacher's goal. Speaking to the listener's heart and mind is the goal. It is listening for their responses and being curious about those responses that leads to spontaneous and natural eye contact, such as is present in any normally flowing conversation, among its participants.

Scripting for speaking can help the preacher remember the action of the sermon and not just its thought. It can help the preacher remember what it is he wants to do in the sermon as well as what is being listened for in the preacher's responses. It can also serve as a graphic reminder that the sermon is not on the page. The sermon, rather, is the actual dynamic human engagement of the hearts and minds of the one who speaks and the several who listen and respond. The actual sermon is never the written words that the preacher has placed on the printed page. It is rather, as Fred Craddock has named it, with honor, that "self-consuming artifact" that gladly expends itself with passion and purpose in the joy of sharing the gospel.

One final practical suggestion for preaching is this: Don't prepare in silence for that which is meant to be spoken aloud. By this I mean don't just think the sermon through or review the script in silence. Speak it out loud and standing up, which is how most preachers will deliver it on Sunday. Perhaps even put it on tape and listen to it a few times. Such methods can strengthen recall and pacing and points of emphasis when the sermon is actually being preached. However, the goal of such oral rehearsal is not polish or memorization. Neither of these qualities is desirable in and of itself. The goal is more simple and direct. It is to set the preacher free to be a faithful, compassionate, present, and responsive servant of the word when he dares to rise and, by God's good grace, speak it from his own heart and mind to the hearts and minds of his listeners come Sunday morning; that is, when he dares to invite them once again to join him on the longest journey any of us will ever in this lifetime attempt to make: the journey from the head to the heart.

# 6

# MAKING THE CONNECTION

∂♪

O Thou who camest from above,
The pure, celestial fire to impart,
Kindle a flame of sacred love
On the mean altar of my heart;
There let it for Thy glory burn.

CHARLES WESLEY
"O Thou Who Camest From Above"

## Preaching and Prayer

Throughout these chapters the goal has been to help preachers, especially my fellow parish pastors, whose responsibility and privilege it is to preach weekly to the same people over an extended period of time often stretching into years, perhaps decades, make the connection between head and heart in their own lives and so also be better equipped to help make that connection in the hearts and minds of their listeners as well. I am convinced that such intentional faithful preaching is an effective aid in meaningful pastoral care and in the nurture of one's own mental and spiritual life as well as the mental and spiritual lives of one's listeners.

At first I thought to include here sermons from persons I consider to be among America's finest contemporary preachers, such as Fred B. Craddock, Eugene Lowry, Barbara Brown Taylor, and Gardner Taylor. But those sermons are already available elsewhere. Besides that, I wanted to present here more realistic examples of what most of us weekly parish preachers might actually be able to do given our capacities and our time constraints and drawing to some degree on our own pastoral experience. So, the two sermons included here are my own. Both of them are from the year in which I've also been writing this book. They are in that sense current to the topic of attempting to make a significant head and heart connection in my own life as well as in the lives of the people I've served as pastor, preaching to them weekly now for seventeen years.

Each sermon begins with a brief introduction, setting the focus and allowing time and space for the listeners to become engaged. The text for the sermon would already have been read earlier in the worship service. In my own Lutheran parish setting this reading occurs just prior to the Children's Sermon, which is then immediately followed by the sermon. I would also have briefly introduced the gospel's context and theme before reading it, as is the custom in many churches these days. Just prior to beginning the sermon I offer a prayer. It is the same prayer each week. The words of this prayer are:

Almighty and Gracious God,
Send out Your Light and Your Truth,
Let them lead us now,
So that the words which are spoken
    and the words which are heard
May be words of the Truth
    of Your Gospel
For the living of our days.
    In Jesus' name. Amen.

This prayer is my own. I believe it is important for every preacher to preface the sermon with some clear invocation of God's presence and guidance and that this invocation be shared with the listeners. It lets them know that the preacher is serious about this matter they are all soon to be engaged in, that the preacher desires the listeners as well as himself to be led by God's Light and Truth, and that it is the preacher's hope that what will be shared now through the sermon, by God's grace, will prove to be helpful both to the listeners and to himself in the living of daily life.

It is, I think, of further help that this presermon prayer be consistently the same. This continuity allows for the regular worshiper to participate silently in the prayer (as some of my listeners have told me they do) and thus also perhaps to be more present to and engaged with the sermon from its outset. They too, after all, have just invoked the presence of God to lead not only the preacher but also themselves. Some such presermon prayer, including intercession for the guidance of the listeners as well as that of the preacher, can be both a sensitive pastoral action, acknowledging the presence and importance of the listeners, and a clear liturgical focusing action for the preacher and the listeners alike.

135

In any event, the specific themes actually addressed in the sermon would likely be more effectively included in the pastoral prayer or the Prayers of the Church later in the service, after these themes have been developed in the sermon and allowed at least some brief time to settle into the listeners own minds and hearts. Having a thoughtful context for such prayer is a distinct advantage encouraging its effectiveness in the church as a praying community of believers in response to the sermon's themes.

An early-twentieth-century preacher, Hans Asmussen, spoke of preaching taking place on the verge of prayer. He said of preaching that it "should be so near to prayer that it would require only a very slight transposition to turn our words into words of prayer."[1] I believe he was right in asserting that the center of the weekly congregational sermon is so much more than the dissemination of interesting, even helpful information; rather, at its center is an act of the preacher's priesthood. The seventeenth-century preacher and poet George Herbert well understood this and expressed it in his own "pre-sermon" prayer:

> Lord Jesus, teach thou me, that I may teach them; sanctify and enable all my powers, that in their full strength they may deliver thy message reverently, readily, faithfully, and fruitfully. O make thy word a swift word, passing from the ear to the heart, from the heart to life and conversation; that as the rain returns not empty, so neither may thy word, but accomplish that for which it is given. O Lord, hear; O Lord, forgive; O Lord, hearken; and do so for thy blessed Son's sake, in whose sweet and pleasing words we say, "Our Father . . ."[2]

These earlier preachers knew the wisdom of tying preaching to prayer and of consciously offering their preaching on the verge of prayer. This relationship between preaching and prayer is equally valid and necessary for us preachers yet today. To follow the example of our forebears in our craft is a wise and faithful thing to do.

## Sermon I: Grace-full Moments
## Sunday: Reformation Sunday
## Text: Romans 3:19-28

*Introduction*: Today the church remembers and celebrates the central tenet of the sixteenth-century Reformation, which remains the vital principle at the heart of Christian theology today: that salvation is by God's grace alone, received through faith—that it is not the work of human hands, lest anyone should boast. This idea did not originate with Martin Luther; rather, he rediscovered what was already present in the teaching of Paul, who was himself quoting the Old Testament prophet Habakkuk, when in Romans Paul writes that "The one who is righteous will live by faith" (Romans 1:17 and Habakkuk 2:4). When Luther read the passage in Romans 3 that is our second reading today, along with Romans 1:17, he wrote in bold letters in the margin of his Bible the words *Sola Gracia*—by grace alone—which have been a cornerstone of Christian gospel proclamation ever since. Yet each new generation must claim the meaning of those words anew in its own time and place if they are to remain vital and vibrant in its own life and not become reduced to an empty slogan devoid of much of anything except a vague remembrance of a once compelling reality. Today's sermon attempts a naming of the presence of grace yet today, with the goal of keeping that presence compelling and encouraging to us now in our own actual time and place. The sermon's title is "Grace-full Moments."

Let us pray:

> Almighty and Gracious God,
> Send out Your Light and Your Truth,
> Let them lead us now,
> So that the words which are spoken
>   and the words which are heard
> May be words of the Truth
>   of Your Gospel
> For the living of our days.
>   In Jesus' name. Amen.

At the start of nearly all his letters, including the epistle to the Romans, grace is what Paul wishes for his friends first—even before he wishes them mercy or peace. He does this, as the contemporary spiritual writer Frederick Buechner reminds us, because he knows that grace is the best thing he can wish for them because grace is the very best thing he himself has ever received.

Paul (whose name at the time was Saul) was on his way to Damascus to round up as many followers of Jesus as he could lay his hands on and bring them back to Jerusalem in chains when he himself received the gift of grace. It was at a totally unexpected time when it most likely seemed to him—confronted as he was by the searing light of God's presence—that what he was going to get was God's judgment. Instead what happened was that God in Christ gave Paul a deeper sense of Paul's own self instead, and he never forgot that grace-full moment for the rest of his life.[3] It was, in fact, the defining moment of his life. (You can read of his experience in the ninth and twenty-second chapters of

Acts.) Many people, however, don't see their own lives as having had such grace-filled moments in them and surely nothing nearly as dramatic as Paul's experience on the Damascus Road. There are those, I'm sure, who see in every cloud only the prospect of unwanted rain while others see there a source of welcomed shade. Some feel only creeping melancholy with each approaching autumn while others see the intense fire of great but fleeting beauty in its dying flowers and plants and leaves. Some see nothing but beauty anywhere and are remarkably insensitive to human suffering and need while others get so obsessed with the world's suffering that they forget the sun rose today.

To keep life in spiritual balance we need to value both rain and shade, to see both beauty and oppression in order not to be deceived, to keep the tension alive between them, our view of life accurate and honest and ourselves fully human. As William Sloane Coffin has written, "When life has that kind of tension in it, it will sing like a violin string."[4] There is, in other words, grace present in our sadness and in our joy, grace present (always) in the fullness of our own human experience as we actually know it—if we train our eyes to see it, our hearts to feel it, our lips and tongues to name it, then we will know better just how blessed our lives are, and have always been, by grace.

When it comes to the mystery of grace we "can do no better than to think about the only case of how it works in the human heart that [we] know intimately and personally, from the inside," and that case is, of course, our own.[5] I believe we've each known some holy, grace-filled moments, even if we've never named them as such. God doesn't leave a single one of our lives untouched by grace, yet how easily and quickly such moments can get lost in the random clutter and busyness of life, how easily overlooked they are, how easily displaced by the "important" things we have to do. Yet when such moments are remembered and named they can become precious, sustaining, healing moments of encouragement and blessing. In naming some such moments of my own I hope some of your own will be evoked in you too.

It's 1956. I'm ten years old. Early one summer morning, with dew on the ground and the mist rising with the sun, I'm pumping as high as I can in a wooden-seated swing at the playground of St. Peter's Lutheran School pretending I'm Audie Murphy bailing out behind German lines on a daring solo mission. I'm trying to best the distance of my last jump, which I've scored with the heel of my child's combat boot in the dirt in front of the swing. I pump high once again and jump, pulling the rip cord on my imaginary parachute as I do, thinking only of World War II glory. I hit the dirt, roll over and for some reason look up into the sky, where between the high puffy white clouds I see a totally uninvited vision of heaven so real to me that I ride my Western Flyer bike home as fast as I can to tell my mother, who is standing in front of the bathroom mirror putting on her makeup before going to work. Both of us are puzzled but neither of us is laughing. She sends me to see Pastor Weise, who doesn't traffic much in visions and gives my experience no credence. He, I imagine, quickly forgot the whole thing. I, in the forty-two years that have passed since then, never have.

It's a few years later and now I'm on the other side of the cyclone fence that divides that playground from Highland View Cemetery. I'm alone again, standing at the freshly sodded grave of my father. As I walk away I smash a tree-limb walking stick fiercely against an elm tree and watch as two of its shattered fragments fly and then fall across each other some distance away into something resembling the form of a cross. A white dove flies overhead and lands in a nearby tree. It doesn't move. Coincidence? Likely so. The need of a young broken heart for reassurance? Yes, definitely. This time I don't tell anyone. But, I remember.

It's over half my lifetime ago now. I'm standing at the mouth of Mitchell Creek where it flows into the Muskegon River near the rapids from which my hometown takes its name. It is a place sacred to me still for the fish I've caught there, the stones I've skipped, the dreams I've dreamed, the prayers I've prayed, the tears I've shed. This time I'm not alone. I'm in the company of a lovely young woman—with a quiver in my voice I ask her to marry me—and she says yes.

Eighteen years later she and I, having rocked an empty cradle for nearly seventeen years of marriage, are waiting together at Gate E-2 at the Philadelphia International Airport at 1:00 A.M. Some of you are there with us. A Northwest Airlines flight from Minnesota, which originated in Seoul, South Korea, arrives, and our infant daughter, whose Korean name, Mee-Wah-Chee, which means "lovely flower," is placed in Linda's arms.

What are such moments as these if not moments full of grace?—moments not so much to be defined as described, not so much to be described as lived and not so much to be lived as to be received as precious gifts of encouragement, meaning, and love.

I believe we each have known such moments. Paul knew them. Martin Luther knew. I have known them. And I believe you have too. But because it is the nature of grace only to fill places that are empty, it is important that we remove some of the clutter and sludge that has accumulated in our hearts and minds across the years so we can see and feel again what once moved us and blessed us so deeply, even if we have never named it.

Someone may perhaps be thinking, "Well that's fine for you, but I've never known such a moment in my life." Well, perhaps, but I still believe you have—that God has not failed to bless you, even when you perhaps often (like me too) haven't attended to such blessings.

> I see a radiant young couple (perhaps last year, perhaps ten or twenty-five or fifty or more years ago), a lovely bride, a then lean, fit groom, standing before an altar and an unknown future. Their hearts are overflowing with love and hope and apprehension. Nervous "I do's" and "I will's" are spoken. Wonder and promise and possibility fill the sanctuary: it is a grace-full moment.
>
> I see a woman and a man together in a birthing room just after their baby's first cry has been heard on this earth; they look into each other's eyes as perhaps they never have before and may never again in quite the same way: it is a grace-full moment.
>
> I see two middle-aged parents sitting in the audience at a high school graduation ceremony while their child—at times not easily raised—walks across the stage to receive a diploma. Without having to look her left hand reaches for his right and they fold together in a long-established way. No words are spoken or needed: it is a grace-full moment.

And I see a woman standing here in this sacred place at her husband's funeral, a man at the funeral of his wife. Tears are flowing as we sing, "For all the saints who from their labors rest," but they aren't all tears of sorrow. There is even the hint of a knowing smile on those wounded faces because deep inside they know that even when it is very hard to confess it, the promise of the resurrection is a true and faithful promise. And so, because they can't sing those words themselves just then, we, their sisters and brothers in Christ, sing the words for them: it is a grace-full moment.

All of these—and so many, many more—are holy moments—moments not without pain, not without perplexity, not without doubt, but also not without grace. This is the great heritage the church celebrates on Reformation Sunday. It is the heritage that knows and confesses that at the heart of every sorrow, at the source of every joy, at the root of every blessing there is grace—always grace—and that where there is grace there is God, and where there is God, we are never alone. And there is nothing closer to the heart of the matter than that.

*Sola Gracia.* By grace alone. Thanks be to God. Amen.

## Sermon II: You Shall Be Mended
### Sunday: Epiphany VI
### Text: Luke 6:17-26

*Introduction*: The great evocative power of the Beatitudes is their naming of some of our core human experiences, none of which is more of a common ground than our mourning. Jesus says of it in today's textual translation, "Blessed are you who weep now, for you will laugh" (Luke 6:21). The spiritual insight offered here is clear and profound: anyone who loves will grieve and will one day also be the object of another's grief. It is the nature of life so to live, and, if loved, so also to die. Today's sermon, "You Shall Be Mended," will focus on this beatitude of mourning, which, in turn, focuses on our most tender, sacred ground: the experience of loss. Let us pray:

> Almighty and Gracious God,
> Send out Your Light and Your Truth,
> Let them lead us now,
> So that the words which are spoken
>     and the words which are heard
> May be words of the Truth
>     of Your Gospel
> For the living of our days.
>     In Jesus' name. Amen.

Just two weeks ago, right here, we conducted the Memorial Service for Good Shepherd's much loved and respected founding pastor, Samuel Besecker. As we sang some of the great hymns of faith, heard the gospel's word of hope and promise read and spoken, and listened to some warm personal reminiscences of Sam's life and ministry, there was many a moist eye here, as well there should have been. Sam was a faithful and compassionate and loving pastor all his days, and his loss was grieved by many who loved him in return.

Those who take the risks of loving will know one kind of sorrow at its loss: the sorrow of pain. Those who don't take such risks will look back one day and know another kind of sorrow: the sorrow of regret. The sorrow of pain is, I believe, much to be preferred. It is a far more noble sorrow no matter how much it hurts.

At Pastor Besecker's graveside service at the Coble Family Cemetery near Chambersburg, Pennsylvania, many more tears were shed, as they have been for generations in that place dating back to the seventeenth century. There are some who glibly tell us how wrong it is for believing Christians to weep before that gaping abyss of the newly dug grave of a loved one, reasoning that faith in the resurrection precludes such weeping. I understand their thinking but I also believe them to be profoundly wrong. Those who weep at the graveside of a dear friend or loved one join the company of Jesus, who wept at the news of his friend Lazarus; they join the company of King David, who wept when his son Absalom died; they join the company of Rachel and all the daughters of Zion, who would not be consoled, weeping at the shallow graves of their children; they join the company of many of our dear friends here, who have wept at their own final leave-taking of loved ones never to be held close or heard or seen again on this earth.

Those who tell us not to weep at the loss of the love we have risked sorrow for, even though well-intentioned, are misguided and offer us no helpful counsel. Whatever else our hope in the resurrection might mean to us, our loss in the present moment of life is often deeply wrenching and without parallel in our experience.

Our human losses can be both powerful and painful, and death is not the only loss we know. During a full lifetime we accumulate a mix of subtle, intangible losses to accompany our more profound ones. The bittersweet loss and gain of a much loved daughter's joyful wedding day, the leave-taking of a forward-looking son hell-bent for college or career, the breakdown of a marriage once full of promise. Once limber joints stiffen; once keen eyesight blurs; energy dissipates more quickly than it once did; memory lapses occur more frequently; the capacity for concentration slackens. Some lose friends; some lose health; some lose dreams; some lose hope. If we live normal lives, we will lose time and time again. It is the nature of a human life, fully lived, to know both the joy and the sorrow of truly loving someone and of making oneself vulnerable to the risks of such loving. Yet no authentic human love is truly possible without such risks. Jesus surely knew this and yet he took the risks involved in loving anyway and he calls us to do the same.

If we love we will also mourn. We will mourn in the graveyard and we will mourn for all those other losses too, each of them stinging the heart and yet also being woven into the whole fabric of the life that we are weaving and will yet present one day to God.

Yet even in the midst of mourning we have the tender promise of Jesus to hold on to: blessed are those who mourn, for they shall be comforted. It is God's own promise that loss and sorrow do not have the final word. That word belongs only to God, who spoke it into the silence of Jesus' own tomb, and although I hear it as three whispered words on Easter morning, the heavens themselves shook with the authority of those words. God whispered, "Rise, my Son," and Jesus did, and the great hope of our own mourning was given birth.

Today's translation has the beatitude translated as, "Blessed are you who weep now, for you will laugh." Another variant substitutes the word *dance* for the word *laugh*. Whatever the translation, the message is clear and good news: mourning never has the final word; God does.

Once there was a preschool-aged boy who, along with the other children, was making a Father's Day present. He was quite excited about it because he loved his daddy very much and wanted to do something special for him. Finally he decided. He would make a very special bowl to hold his daddy's coins and keys and pocketknife at night. He and his teacher carefully formed and fired the clay, and the next day, after it had cooled, they prepared to paint it. The boy was very deliberate in making his color selection. He finally settled on red because red was his daddy's favorite color. So he lovingly painted the bowl red, biting his lower lip in concentration as he did so and applying red paint liberally to his pudgy fingers and smock as well.

The Friday before Father's Day finally arrived and the boy was thrilled that both his mommy and his daddy had made special arrangements to be at the school party that day. Following the program of songs and recitations he was so excited to take his special bowl to his daddy that in his hurry he tripped and fell and the bowl shattered into many pieces on the school's hard-surfaced hallway floor. He sat down among all those red pieces and began to cry. The father, a bit embarrassed by his son's crying, stood over the boy, ruffled the boy's hair and said firmly, "It's all right, son. It doesn't really matter." But the boy's mother, who was much wiser in such things, sat down beside the boy among the pieces of broken red bowl and said, "I know, son. It does matter, doesn't it? It matters very much. It was a beautiful bowl you made for daddy." And together the boy and the mother cried.

After a few minutes their tears subsided and from somewhere deep in that bottomless resource of a mother's purse came some tissue. They wiped their eyes and blew their noses. Then the mother laid out some more tissues on the floor and said, "Now let's pick up all the pieces we can find and take them home and see what we can make out of them." The daddy, having learned a lesson, got down on his knees and helped too.[6]

The wise mother knew, as did Qoheleth in Ecclesiastes, that there is "a time to weep, and a time to laugh; a time to mourn, and a time to dance" (Ecclesiastes 3:4). Any human life fully lived will know sorrow over innumerable other kinds of losses and diminishments too. But as people of faith and of trust in the promises of Jesus, we also know that there comes a time when weeping yields to laughter and mourning to dancing. The Hebrews knew this long ago. When their beloved leader, Moses, died and was buried in a valley in the land of Moab, the people "wept for Moses in the plains of Moab thirty days; then the period of mourning for Moses was ended" (Deuteronomy 34:8). Then God did not leave the people comfortless but raised up Joshua the son of Nun to lead them, and they went on to enter the Promised Land.

The story of the young boy's broken bowl reminds us of this goodness of God, that is, when mourning has run its course it is time to pick up the shattered pieces and begin, in faith and hope, to see what can still be made of them.

In her spiritual journal, *Everyday Sacred,* Sue Bender describes what she calls an imperfectly perfect bowl. She was a novice potter when she saw a strikingly handsome Japanese tea bowl that had been broken and then pieced together. The bowl made a lasting impression on her, because instead of trying to hide the flaws, the wise potter had decided to emphasize the cracks and had filled them with silver, making the broken bowl even more precious and beautiful after it had been mended than it had been before.

Most of us have lived long enough now to know that sometimes our bowls get cracked—even broken. But we also know that sometimes, with time and patience and forgiveness and love, they can be mended and made into things of even greater strength and beauty than they were before—when we offer the unique and precious silver of our own lives and love for the mending.

And sometimes, when the loss is simply too great, the mending can't take place on this earth. But God will yet do the final mending, nevertheless, with the gospel silver of the resurrection of the dead, as in these words, if we might allow ourselves yet another rendering of Jesus' tender, strong promise: Blessed are those who weep, for they shall be mended.

Thanks be to God. Amen.

# Conclusion

These two sermons were attempts of my own to speak intentionally to both the hearts and the minds of my listeners. I imagine I did not do so with some. I hope that I did do so with others. The Holy Spirit will, of course, work as the Holy Spirit wills to work in their lives as in my own. I firmly believe that our task as preachers is to speak to the whole person, to the mind, to the heart, to the memory, to the volition, to the spirit, as thoughtfully and capably as we can. Although life's longest and most arduous journey is surely the one from the head to the heart, it is also life's most deeply rewarding one. It is my hope that I have offered here some encouragement to my fellow preachers in making that journey faithfully, compassionately, and well in their own lives and in their preaching.

I believe Frederick Buechner to have been right when in *Longing for Home* he wrote, "Not to speak from the heart of where . . . faith comes from is to risk never really touching the hearts of those . . . who so hungrily listen."[7] So to speak and so to be heard must surely be

**149**

one of the preacher's deepest blessings. May it be true for us all. Godspeed to you, my fellow preacher, on the journey. May you travel safely, wisely, deeply, and well. Borrowing that wonderful salutation from Alan Paton's *Cry, The Beloved Country,* I conclude: Go well. Stay well.

# POSTSCRIPT

## THE PREACHER'S KITCHEN WORK

♪♪

In the Danish film *Babbette's Feast,* a flurry of intense activity takes place in the close confines of a simple, unadorned country kitchen. Pots are boiling, knives flashing, pans clattering as Babbette, who had been one of France's finest chefs (although this fact is unknown in the small Danish village where she now resides in exile), creates a meal of delectable French cuisine for the unsuspecting, dour guests seated in the dining room. The guests, however, see none of the intense preparations taking place in the kitchen. They see and experience only the wonderful meal that is set before their eyes. This is as it should be. The cooking pots don't belong on the dining table with the fine china. Just so, neither do abstract statements of theology or all of the preacher's appropriately hidden labor of preparation. Only the finest fare should be brought from the kitchen to the finely dressed table. Most of the preacher's hard labor ought to take place in private and remain unseen to the listener's eyes and unheard by the listener's ears. Just as the virtuoso violinist doesn't practice scales while in concert performance, so too ought the preacher leave much of the hard work done behind at the study desk, carrying only the jewels of thought and imagination from that labor into the pulpit. This requires of the preacher the great but necessary discipline of restraint, that is, the ability not to share everything she knows or has learned about a topic but only that which she has discerned, through hard work, disciplined study, and earnest prayer, to be most truly helpful and gospel centered. This unseen and unacknowledged kitchen work of the preacher's craft is indeed demanding, but its importance is hard to overestimate because its direct beneficiaries are those unsuspecting listeners who, like those unsuspecting Danes at Babbette's feast, sit at the preacher's table and, by God's grace, discover there a very fine meal indeed.

The final word I yield to the preacher and poet George MacDonald, who, weary in mind and spirit by the costliness of his own preaching, offers this earnest, telling prayer:

O Lord, I have been talking to the people;
Thoughts' wheels have round me whirled a fiery zone,
And the recoil of my words' airy ripple
My heart unheedful has puffed up and blown.
Therefore I cast myself before thee prone:
Lay cool hands on my burning brain, and press
From my weak heart the swelling emptiness.
—George MacDonald
*Diary of an Old Soul*

# NOTES

⚜

## Preface

1. Frederick Buechner, *The Longing for Home: Recollections and Reflections* (San Francisco: HarperCollins, 1996), p. 177.

2. George MacDonald, *Ranald Bannerman's Boyhood,* quoted in *The Wind from the Stars: Through the Year with George MacDonald,* ed. Gordon Reid (London: HarperCollins Religious, 1992), 63.

3. Evelyn Hopper, *Life of Evelyn Underhill* (New York: Harper and Brothers, 1958), p. 75.

4. Larry McMurtry, *Lonesome Dove* (New York: Pocket Books, 1985), p. 235.

## Chapter 1: The Importance of the Head and Heart Connection

1. Saul Bellow, *Humboldt's Gift* (New York: Penguin Books, 1984), p. 441.

2. James Stalker, in Alexander Gammie, *Preachers I Have Heard* (Glasgow: Pickering & Inglis, 1946), pp. 45-46, quoted in *Minister's Prayer Book,* ed. John W. Doberstein (Philadelphia: Fortress Press, 1959), p. 184.

3. David Keirsey and Marilyn Bates, *Please Understand Me: Character and Temperament Types,* 5th ed. (Del Mar, Ca.: Prometheus Nemesis, 1984), pp. 1-26.

4. Edward Farley, "Toward Theological Understanding: An Interview with Edward Farley," *The Christian Century* 115 (4-11 February 1998): 114.

5. George Tyrrell, *Oil and Wine* (1907), p. xii, quoted in *A Diary of Readings,* ed. John Baillie (New York: Charles Scribner's Sons, 1955), Day 62.

6. John Watson, *The Cure of Souls* (New York: Dodd, Mead, 1896), p. 224, quoted in *Minister's Prayer Book,* p. 357.

## Notes

### Chapter 2: The Person in the Pulpit: Integrity, Authenticity, and Authority in Preaching to Head and Heart

1. Johann Michael Sailer, quoted in *Minister's Prayer Book*, ed. John W. Doberstein (Philadelphia: Fortress Press, 1959), p. 272.
2. Richard Baxter, *The Reformed Pastor*, The Practical Works of the Rev. Richard Baxter, vol. 14 (1830), p. 55, quoted in *Minister's Prayer Book*, p. 266.
3. Emily Dickinson, quoted in Kathleen Norris, *Amazing Grace: A Vocabulary of Faith* (New York: Riverhead Books, 1998), p. 249.
4. Hans van der Geest, *Presence in the Pulpit: The Impact of Personality in Preaching* (Atlanta: John Knox Press, 1981), pp. 27-28.
5. Kathleen Norris, *Amazing Grace*, p. 141.
6. Harris W. Lee, *Effective Church Leadership: A Practical Sourcebook* (Minneapolis: Augsburg Fortress, 1989), p. 75.
7. Fred B. Craddock, *Preaching* (Nashville: Abingdon Press, 1985), p. 24.
8. Jackson W. Carroll, *As One With Authority: Reflective Leadership in Ministry* (Louisville: Westminster/John Knox Press, 1991), p. 38.
9. Urban T. Holmes III, *The Priest in Community: Exploring the Roots of Ministry* (New York: Seabury Press, 1978), pp. 176, 67.
10. Jackson W. Carroll, *As One With Authority*, p. 47.
11. Hans van der Geest, *Presence*, pp. 52-55.
12. Herman Melville, *Moby Dick* (New York: Bantam Books, 1981), p. 46.

### Chapter 3: Valuing the Listener: Curiosity and Indefiniteness in Addressing the Head and the Heart

1. Harold S. Kushner, *Who Needs God?* (New York: Pocket Books, 1989), pp. 165-66.
2. Ibid., p. 166.
3. George MacDonald, *Ranald Bannerman's Boyhood*, quoted in *The Wind from the Stars: Through the Year with George MacDonald*, ed. Gordon Reid (London: HarperCollins Religious, 1992), 63.
4. Kathleen Norris, *Amazing Grace: A Vocabulary of Faith* (New York: Riverhead Books, 1998), pp. 162-63.
5. R. E. C. Browne, *The Ministry of the Word* (Philadelphia: Fortress Press, 1976), p. 59.
6. Ibid., p. 66.
7. *Letters from Baron von Hügel to a Niece*, ed. Gwendolen Greene (J. M. Dent & Sons, 1928), p. xvi, quoted in R. E. C. Browne, *Ministry*, p. 58.

### Chapter 4: How to Develop the Head and Heart Connection

1. Wilhelm Löhe, *The Lutheran Pastor*, trans. G. H. Gerberding, pp. 202-3,

quoted in *Minister's Prayer Book*, ed. John W. Doberstein (Philadelphia: Fortress Press, 1959), pp. 279-80.

2. Garrison Keillor, *Listening for God: Contemporary Literature and the Life of Faith* (Minneapolis: Augsburg Fortress Video, 1994).

3. Kathleen Norris, *Amazing Grace: A Vocabulary of Faith* (New York: Riverhead Books, 1998), pp. 242-43.

4. Linda Swears, *Teaching the Elementary School Chorus* (New York: Parker Publishing Company, 1984), p. 50.

5. Elton Trueblood, *The New Man for Our Time* (New York: Harper & Row, 1970), p. 69, quoted in Rueben P. Job and Norman Shawchuck, *A Guide to Prayer for Ministers and Other Servants* (Nashville: The Upper Room, 1983), pp. 226-27.

6. For a fuller development of the principles presented here see Craddock's books *Preaching* (Nashville: Abingdon Press, 1985), *As One Without Authority* (Nashville: Abingdon Press, 1979), and *Overhearing the Gospel* (Nashville: Abingdon Press, 1978). Unfortunately Phil Swander died in 1986 before he was able to commit much of his thought to writing. References to his work in this book come from my experience of being instructed by him in classroom and tutored by him in private session.

7. Keillor, *Listening for God*.

8. For a fuller presentation of the relationship between sermon development and narrative art form see Lowry's books *The Homiletical Plot: The Sermon as Narrative Art Form* (Atlanta: John Knox Press, 1980); *Doing Time in the Pulpit: The Relationship Between Narrative and Preaching* (Nashville: Abingdon Press, 1985), and more recently, *The Sermon: Dancing the Edge of Mystery* (Nashville: Abingdon Press, 1997).

9. Eugene Lowry, *The Homiletical Plot*, pp. 22-25.

10. John Ruskin, quoted in Newell Hillis, *Great Men as Prophets of a New Era* (New York: Revell, 1922), pp. 212-13, quoted in *Minister's Prayer Book*, pp. 397-98.

11. Marcus Borg, "Postmodern Revisioning," *Christian Century* 114 (5 November 1997): 1013, quoted in Kathleen Norris, *Amazing Grace*, p. 190.

12. Kathleen Norris, *Amazing Grace*, p. 120.

13. Ibid.

14. Eugene H. Peterson, *Subversive Spirituality* (Grand Rapids: Eerdmans, 1997), pp. 252-53.

15. Thomas Cahill, *The Gifts of the Jews: How a Tribe of Desert Nomads Changed the Way Everyone Thinks and Feels* (New York: Nan A. Talese Doubleday, 1998), p. 49.

16. Saul Bellow, *Humboldt's Gift* (New York: Penguin Books, 1984), p. 437.

17. George MacDonald, *Ranald Bannerman's Boyhood*, quoted in *The Wind from the Stars: Through the Year with George MacDonald*, ed. Gordon Reid (London: HarperCollins Religious, 1992), 63.

18. Barbara Brown Taylor, *The Preaching Life* (Cambridge, Ma.: Cowley Publications, 1993), p. 39.

19. Ibid., pp. 39-40.

20. Gail Ramshaw, *God Beyond Gender: Feminist Christian God-Language* (Philadelphia: Fortress Press, 1994), p. 97.

21. Paul Ricoeur, cited in Richard L. Eslinger, *Narrative and Imagination,* (Minneapolis: Fortress Press, 1995), p. 67, quoted in Eugene Lowry, *The Sermon,* p. 64.

22. Evans E. Crawford, *The Hum: Call and Response in African American Preaching* (Nashville: Abingdon Press, 1995), p. 50, quoted in Eugene Lowry, *The Sermon,* p. 72.

## Chapter 5: Communicating the Head and Heart Connection Effectively

1. Hans van der Geest, *Presence in the Pulpit: The Impact of Personality in Preaching* (Atlanta: John Knox Press, 1981), p. 57.

2. Kathleen Norris, *Amazing Grace: A Vocabulary of Faith* (New York: Riverhead Books, 1998), p. 253.

3. The basis for these practical principles was developed during time spent in tutorial and workshop sessions with J. Phillip Swander, who taught communications at Union Theological Seminary and at Hebrew Union College in New York City for thirteen years in addition to being the director of the Auburn Theological Seminary's Biblical Preaching Project in the Susquehanna Valley of New York State. He also conducted workshops on oral/aural communications throughout the country. Unfortunately he died before he was able to commit his creative, thoughtful work to full manuscript form.

4. Douglas Steere, *Together in Solitude* (New York: Crossroad Publishing, 1982), p. 124.

5. R. E. C. Browne, *The Ministry of the Word* (Philadelphia: Fortress Press, 1976), p. 97.

6. J. Phillip Swander, "Action in the Art of Preaching," *The Auburn News,* Spring 1986, p. 1.

7. Ibid., p. 2.

8. Ibid., p. 3.

9. Ibid., p. 4.

10. Ibid, p. 2.

11. The concept of scripting was presented by Swander both at preaching conferences at the College of Preachers, National Cathedral, Washington, D.C., in 1982 and 1985, and in private tutorial sessions with him in New York City.

## Chapter 6: Making the Connection

1. Hans Asmussen, letter to pastors, 7 July 1948, quoted in *Minister's Prayer Book,* ed. John W. Doberstein (Philadelphia: Fortress Press, 1959), p. 297.

2. George Herbert, *The Temple & A Priest in the Temple,* Everyman's Library (London: Dent), p. 292, quoted in *Minister's Prayer Book,* pp. 138-39.

3. Frederick Buechner, *The Longing for Home: Recollections and Reflections* (San Francisco: HarperCollins, 1996), p. 175.

**156**

4. William Sloane Coffin, *Order of Saints Martin and Teresa Journal* (October-December 1998): 5 (Oct. 14th Reading).

5. Frederick Buechner, *Longing for Home,* p. 176.

6. Adapted from William Muehl, *Why Preach? Why Listen?* (Philadelphia: Fortress Press, 1986), p. 92.

7. Buechner, *Longing for Home,* p. 177.